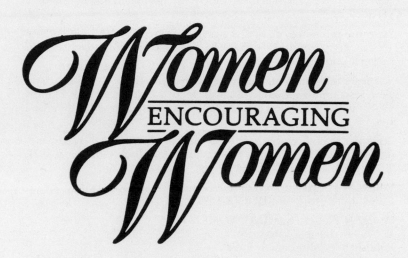

Women Encouraging Women

Lucibel VanAtta

MULTNOMAH

Unless otherwise indicated, all Scripture references are from the Holy Bible: New International Version, copyright 1973, 1978, 1984, by the International Bible Society. Used by permission of Zondervan Bible Publishers.

Scripture references marked TLB are taken from The Living Bible, copyright 1971 by Tyndale House Publishers, Wheaton, Ill. Used by permission.

Scripture references marked Amplified are from The Amplified New Testament, copyright 1954, 1958 by The Lockman Foundation. Used by permission.

Scripture references marked Phillips are from the J. B. Phillips: The New Testament in Modern English, revised edition. © J. B. Phillips 1958, 1960, 1972. Used by permission of Macmillan Publishing Co., Inc.

Scripture references marked NASB are from the New American Standard Bible, © The Lockman Foundation 1960, 1962, 1963, 1968, 1971, 1972, 1973, 1975, 1977. Used by permission.

Edited by Liz Heaney
Cover design by Bruce DeRoos

WOMEN ENCOURAGING WOMEN
© 1987 by Lucibel Van Atta
Published by Multnomah Press

Printed in the United States of America

Library of Congress Cataloging in Publication Data

Van Atta, Lucibel.
   Women encouraging women.

   Bibliography: p.
   1. Women—Religious life.   2. Bible. N.T. Titus II,
3-5—Criticism, interpretation, etc.   I. Title.
BV4527.v36   1988   248.8'43   87-28264
ISBN 0-88070-214-1 (pbk.)

93 94 95 – 10 9 8 7 6 5

To Bob

My constant encourager
and my spiritual
mentor for over
forty years

"One generation will commend your works to another;
they will tell of your mighty acts."
Psalm 145:4

"Likewise, teach the older women to be reverent in
the way they live, not to be slanderers or addicted
to much wine, but to teach what is good.
Then they can train the younger women to love
their husbands and children, to be self-controlled
and pure, to be busy at home, to be kind, and to
be subject to their husbands, so that no one will
malign the word of God."

Titus 2:3-5

CONTENTS

TO THE READER

Three years after my first mentoring relationship, an idea began to simmer in my mind. Could I share in depth what I had learned from my experiences with young women like Marni and Stephanie? Could I also pass along the lessons of my patient mentor, the Lord Jesus Christ? With each positive and encouraging response I received, from discipling articles I've written and workshops I've given, God seemed to affirm the need for this book.

I have changed names and some details of actual experiences to purposely frustrate any guessing games about identities. Thank you for understanding that I can in no way violate the trust of my discipling friends.

At the conclusion of each chapter in this book the Worthy Woman Ideas are designed to give you something to *do* about what you have just read. Although our busy lives usually preclude jumping at the chance to take on anything more, trying at least a few of these "ideas" could make a significant difference in your progress as one of God's worthy women. I'm usually a little frustrated by lines which don't match up to what I want to write, so you won't find lines or spaces in the book for following up on Worthy Woman ideas. I've liked using my personal notebook to work out any lists or thinking-through comments, but choose whatever method you like.

Now join me, reader-friend, in this exploration of a life-shaping adventure!

1

WHO WILL DISCIPLE ME?

———————————————————————————

The letter slid out from between bills and advertisements in my mailbox. The introductory words startled me: "I was stunned by the thought that older women are to teach the younger women to love their husbands. *Being taught to love was a totally new idea!*"

I knew the writer of this letter only by sight. Marni* was a young married woman in our church. Like many of the women I've nurtured and discipled, Marni's family lived

* Names and some details have been changed throughout this book to maintain privacy.

thousands of miles away. But the command she discovered in Titus 2:3-5 nudged her to recognize she needed a mentor.

While her husband prepared for ministry in Christian education, she wanted someone to equip her for the lifestyle of a godly woman. Her letter continued:

> As I thought about this biblical command, I realized the advantages for a young married woman who followed through on this principle. I began looking at all the mature women with years of experience in marriage, in handling problems, and in learning to love. The Lord encouraged me to seek out a woman whom I respect as a wife; one who could teach me to love my husband.
>
> Last Sunday I decided to put these thoughts before you and see if you would be willing to disciple me.

Several days of prayer and uncertainty followed. Since my hours and days seemed more than full already, I stumbled again and again over Marni's request. But a familiar section of the gospels—where Jesus fed so many with so little—finally pushed aside my "sanctified rationalizing." Those incredible leftovers Jesus used spoke louder to me than any sermon, and I began to understand the difference between *His* blessing and my logic.

After discussing the idea with my husband, I said yes to Marni's request, and I began leaning harder on the Lord than at any previous time.

WOMEN NEED ONE ANOTHER

When Marni expressed her need to learn to love, she unknowingly represented most of the other seminary and college wives I spent time with later. I asked her one day why she and other young women with good Christian families needed role models and mentors. As she pondered my question, Marni's forefinger traced a pattern on the tablecloth so precisely it seemed she expected a pop quiz at any moment.

She finally replied that the most basic reason went back to the Fall, and the broken relationships that have resulted ever since. Marni spoke of the bitterness felt by some of her peers over mistakes they felt their parents made with them. Then she told me some of their thoughts:

"I could never talk to my mother because she was so pious and legalistic."

"I don't respect what my parents say because they didn't act it out in their lives."

"When I try to be all things to all people, I end up expecting too much of myself. I feel sometimes I'm walking the tightrope of other people's expectations—especially when I'm confronted with the yearly hassle of 'which parents do we visit this year for the holidays?'"

Another young friend said simply, "The reasons are as varied as the women and their relationships with their parents. But the important thing is finding older women friends to look up to, even if we seem to have blown it with our own parents."

Other young women who have had healthy experiences and relationships with their parents say things such as:

"I just want to learn how to be a godly woman."

"I don't really enjoy hospitality, and I wonder if I could learn some tips to make it easier."

"I want someone who can help me think through some goals and hold me accountable for personal growth."

In recent years I've seen more and more women searching—consciously or unconsciously—for contemporary yet biblical ways to be better "keepers at home." Most of today's Christian women want to live out their beliefs, but aren't always sure how to make this happen.

I believe God's time is *now* for rediscovering His Titus 2:3-5 principle:

> Likewise, teach the older women to be reverent in the way they live, not to be slanderers or addicted to much wine, but to teach what is good. Then they can train the younger women to love their husbands and children, to be self-controlled and pure, to be busy at home, to be kind, and to be subject to their husbands, so that no one will malign the word of God.

Mothers and female relatives remain the time-honored and natural choices for role models. But too many miles or transient lifestyles or broken family relationships may separate them from us. Many young women in the 1980s long for a hiding place from life's storms and look for someone who will bend down to listen and help bear the burdens that press so fiercely upon them.

Christian women today are looking for mentors.

WOMEN WITH SPECIAL NEEDS FOR MENTORING

One pastor told me, "If every mature Christian woman took just one less mature Christian woman for about two years—parenting her, walking alongside her, seeing her do the same for others—exciting things would happen in this church."

He was referring particularly to the needs of new or un-committed Christians, but I'm convinced that every woman needs a role model for the different stages and changepoints of her life.

My friend Maggie benefited from a discipling relationship when she returned to college before assuming a demanding but satisfying full-time career. She had been a full-time homemaker, mother, wife, and church worker all through her twenties, thirties, and forties. Because of the abrupt changes in Maggie's lifestyle and priorities, she needed a mentor to ease the trauma of transition.

The thirty-fifth birthday of my friend Shelley precipitated almost a year of unhealthy doubts about where she was headed with her life. She was discontented with her singleness. Slowly I helped her realign her expectations and her perspective so that she had a clearer view of how to gain a sense of purpose and meaning.

All of us need mentoring at specific and crucial points in our lives. However, there are women whose situations accentuate their need for a mentor. I'd like to highlight a few.

Women from non-Christian homes. New and younger Christians seldom grow significantly through a church program. They need one-on-one discipling.

The woman without parents or husband to share her Christian convictions certainly needs an older Christian woman to nurture and teach her about godly qualities such as self-control and purity. She needs someone to confide in and pray with. Through the years I've almost taken for granted the simple fact that I can ask my family to pray for me. Many women never know that blessed privilege and support.

Women with emotional hurts. Many women suffer emotionally. Some women, like Fran, have experienced sexual and emotional abuse as a child. Perhaps they have worked overtime at pleasing men (this was Fran's only way of getting attention as a child), but find themselves without any familiar props after accepting God's offer of salvation in Christ. Others live with a poor choice of mate or job or church responsibility or friends. I've known women who live with a lack of love every day of their lives or the fallout from an insensitive or overbearing employer or husband or parents. When a woman discovers she or a loved one has cancer or some life threatening illness, her emotional stability is strained. Those whose hurt stems from divorce, job loss, abuse, infidelity, or poverty often suffer silently.

These women need to be encouraged.

Women without mothers. Women who have lost their mothers need an "adopted mom." Becky did. She came from a solid family background but her mother died shortly before Becky's tenth birthday. Twenty years later she felt her loss anew. In some ways I became the spiritual mom and mentor Becky lacked.

I tried to remain available for the "trivial" concerns of her life as well as the "biggies." And I listened. Becky recognized her need for someone who could point her questions and quaverings back to God's Word, the ultimate sounding board.

I also provided the dual nourishing and nudging that birth mothers instinctively give. Sometimes this came by just giving a generational perspective to what Becky was going through. It helped her, for instance, to realize that her oldest child wouldn't suck her thumb forever.

For Becky and others I also want to model God's concept of a worthy woman. These women need to see a woman live out the specifics of Scripture such as 1 Peter 3:3-4, which talks about the kind of beauty that comes from within rather than from fancy jewelry or stylish haircuts or expensive clothes.

Widows and single parents. Some widows are barely twenty or thirty and are struggling to rear their children alone. Those of us whose children are grown can nurture and mentor a single mom or a young widow by lovingly offering her some of our time and resources.

In Psalm 146:8-9 God expresses His deep concern for widows and other lonely women: "The LORD loves the righteous. The LORD watches over the alien and sustains the fatherless and the widow." I believe He wants you and me to express concern through our acts of love toward these women who have such an urgent need for caring support.

And their need is not only for woman-to-woman discipling, but for a break from being endlessly on call with young children. This may become too much for one mentor to handle. Perhaps a concerned and godly man will volunteer as an "adopted" daddy; at times your husband or a friend might join forces with you.

You and I can best help the single mom by meeting that woman at her greatest point of need. Judy needed someone to help her pull away from a strong dependence on television soaps. Encouraging Judy to spend more time in God's Word rather than languishing in front of the TV was a long-range project which eventually led to a more godly lifestyle.

Single women. Single women need mentoring, too. Many need to realize that their worth does not depend on being either married or single. They need disciplemakers who will reinforce this truth and who will also become loyal friends. They need women who will affirm and hold them accountable to live godly lives.

Single women need more than just the "good Christian fellowship" churches are finally beginning to provide. Sometimes their desire for ministry gets overlooked or sidetracked in our local churches. Many are gifted in the areas of administration, teacher training, leading group discussions, or counseling. Others work effectively with college or international students or in camping and retreat programs. Single women are needed to counsel other singles, to work with children, to lead Bible studies, or just to be with other families on weekends. These women need to be encouraged to reach their potential, to enjoy ministry, and to get to know the rest of the church family.

Sometimes a young woman just wants to talk through her feelings and discoveries and goals. This was true of Kristin. As we met together to pray one afternoon, she admitted to a deteriorating relationship with her mother. When she detailed her mom's unreasonable expectations, I began to understand and sensed that Kristin feared rejection from her mother more than she feared rejection from anyone else.

That day I mostly listened as Kristin unburdened her heart. But when she started out the door I remember drawing her close with a hug and seeing her smile when I suggested: "I suspect that you need another mom these days, a spiritual mom to fill in some of the cracks in your relationship with your own mom. Could I candidate for that spot?"

Since most single women will marry, they need to know what the Bible teaches about being a godly wife and mother. Kristin and I met together weekly at the conclusion of her fourth grade teaching day. We zeroed in on goals she had previously written down. One of them stated: "preparation for the possibility of marriage someday." Two years later God's handpicked man met and married her. Now that Kristin is a wife and homemaker, she is able to see the relevance of what we discussed and studied. Our times together helped prepare her for marriage.

Women in leadership. Women who minister in leadership positions need nurturing and encouragement, just like the rest of us. MaeBelle King is one of those winsome ladies from the South; the kind who could charm the fuzz right off a Georgia peach. I attended a meeting where MaeBelle shared some of her experiences and insights about spiritual mothers. Here is what she said:

> When I first became a pastor's wife I felt I didn't have much to contribute to the church. I considered the church quite fortunate to get my husband, but felt I lacked talent and confidence.
>
> Just as a natural mother instinctively knows when her child is hurting, a lady in our church knew that I felt inadequate. One day she sent me a note in the mail, assuring me that my contribution was needed and important—even though it wasn't highly visible.
>
> By encouraging and nurturing, she nudged me to become more of what God wanted me to be. And God used this spiritual mother in my life over and over again.

At this point MaeBelle let us know that when she talked about spiritual mothers she referred to discipleship—one woman nurturing and nudging another woman in her spiritual walk.

She urged those who felt like "spiritual orphans" to look for the spiritual mom God would provide:

> She won't necessarily have gray hair; possibly she is your contemporary. But she is someone who can help you take your place in the chain of discipleship

Paul spoke of in 1 Thessalonians, "But we were gentle among you, like a mother caring for her little children. We loved you so much that we were delighted to share with you not only the gospel of God but our lives as well, because you had become so dear to us . . . encouraging, comforting and urging you to live lives worthy of God, who calls you into his kingdom and glory" (2:7-8, 12).

I hope the words of this pastor's wife have nudged *you* to consider becoming an encourager to a woman in leadership—or to whomever God leads you.

COMMITMENT TO GOD MEANS COMMITMENT TO HIS FAMILY

Don't be overwhelmed by the mentoring we've suggested here. My prayer is that you will approach this book with a mindset that asks, "I wonder if the Lord wants to use me in this kind of relationship?"

We who are older (and we're all older than someone else!) have a beautiful opportunity to encourage our younger friends in developing and cultivating ministries of their own; to gently push them into new situations—slightly beyond their present depth—which enable them to trust God totally. How sad if any young woman should stub her toe on our indifference!

Commitment to God requires commitment to God's people. Because God's plan—past, present, future—is always wrapped around people. "One generation shall praise Thy works to another, and shall declare Thy mighty acts" (Psalm 145:4, NASB).

Mentoring isn't just another activity to scrunch into our already over-crowded calendars. It is a relationship, a commitment, and a step of faith. A faith defined as giving God the opportunity to fulfill His promise through our lives. And this is indeed what pleases God.

"And without faith it is impossible to please God" (Hebrews 11:6).

WORTHY WOMAN IDEAS

1. List the women you know who, for different reasons, seem to need nurturing. You may want to include yourself. Find specific Scriptures which address their hurts and needs.

2. Read Ephesians 1:3-14 and note carefully all God has done for you and who you are because He has done these things. How can you share these truths to encourage and support someone who needs affirming?

3. Write down some specific ways you can encourage and support women you know who are in leadership positions. Perhaps you will select some acts of lovingkindness; perhaps you will include more difficult assignments, such as pulling down the unrealistic expectations of a pastor's wife. Could you become a spiritual daughter or mother to a pastor's wife?

2

WHO CAN MENTOR?

———————————————————————

Although I didn't expect all the questions Sharla tossed at me after church that Sunday, I delighted in her evident interest.

"Am I too young to disciple my friend Emily? I'm afraid I'm not quite spiritual enough to be a role model . . . what if I find that it takes more time that I can give?"

I, too, struggled for quite a while with the concept of being either a role model or mentor. For me those terms pictured someone on a higher level, someone to be looked up to as an ideal—a heroine. Because I associate mentoring with the educational and business worlds, I still cringe a little when I'm linked with those words, feeling a bit of an imposter.

But I've added these biblically valid words—*role model* and *mentor*—to my vocabulary and lifestyle, and they seem to fit better these days. I've discovered that a mentor is "someone close and trusted and experienced."

Mentoring requires no special talent or God-given quality. All God asks is for us to take seriously the task of nurturing and building up other women. In her book, *Out of the Saltshaker*, Rebecca Manley Pippert underscores this truth. She urges us to do what we can with who we are:

> We must not wait until we are healed first, loved first, and then reach out. We must serve no matter how little we have our act together. It may well be that one of the first steps toward our own healing will come when we reach out to someone else.[1]

THE BIBLICAL DESCRIPTION

What, then, is required of a mentor?

Let's look again at Paul's words: "Likewise, teach the older women to be reverent in the way they live, not to be slanderers or addicted to much wine, but to teach what is good" (Titus 2:3).

Older. What does Paul mean by *older*? Does he mean women in the grandmother category?

Throughout his writing, Paul sets forth the biblical principle of the older woman as a godly role model—nurturing and assuming responsibility for the younger woman. He probably categorizes more than he sets age limits.

In most cases the mentor's chronological age will add up to at least a few years older than the woman she disciples. I believe the woman with greater spiritual experience and maturity also qualifies as "older" in the Lord. These women have previously accepted responsibility and accountability for their Christian experience.

Thus, even a woman in her twenties can effectively mentor someone younger. For several months a high school junior sang alongside a college woman in our church choir before asking her for regular nurturing. What had begun very tentatively and informally grew easily into a loosely structured relationship of lasting value.

Young couples sometimes "adopt" one or more high school or college students, encouraging and welcoming them to a "home away from home." Craig and Carolyn did this before twin girl babies took over a major chunk of their lives. But one high school girl stayed with that relationship. She wanted more time around Carolyn, her role model. Lisa helped Carolyn with the babies in many ways and benefited from her on-the-spot nurturing.

Reverent in behavior. Because Paul didn't want any doubt about the Titus 2:3 mentoring prerequisite, he spelled it out for us: "reverent in the way they live." We are to have a lifestyle worthy of respect at all times.

Paul used the compound Greek word *hiero-prepei* which relates to "actions sacred to God" and suggests an appropriately honorable behavior. I'm reminded of the woman of worth pictured for us in Proverbs 31:26-30:

> She speaks with wisdom,
>   and faithful instruction is on her tongue.
> She watches over the affairs of her household
>   and does not eat the bread of idleness.
> Her children arise and call her blessed;
>   her husband also, and he praises her:
> "Many women do noble things,
>   but you surpass them all."
> Charm is deceptive, and beauty is fleeting;
>   but a woman who fears the LORD is
>   to be praised.

A woman who merely *says* the right Christian words won't qualify as a discipler. We are talking honorable living, day in and day out. Today's godly woman does not flaunt her reverent behavior, but it always shows through—in the careful and caring ways she listens to people of all ages; in her discreet but attractive appearance which mirrors her inner beauty; in her respect for others and their feelings; and in all her relationships.

Able to keep confidences. Titus 2 pays special mention to the problem of talking about other people. Because some older women have a poor track record for keeping confidences under lock and key, many younger women avoid settling into a mentoring relationship. Disciplemakers must have nothing to do with gossip or idle talk or rumors.

These two examples of Solomon's heavy warning about the tongue in Proverbs may whet your appetite for further reading there:

> Wise [women] store up knowledge, but the mouth
> of a fool invites ruin (10:14).

> Pleasant words are a honeycomb, sweet to the soul
> and healing to the bones (16:24).

One can count unconditionally on a Titus 2 woman. She values discernment and integrity.

I suspect that whether younger or older we've all been tempted to reveal something we shouldn't. *Now, what true-to-life illustration can I use to clinch my words?* we subconsciously wonder. But bringing out in the open even the tiniest bit of someone else's life shatters their trust and your integrity. If you or I try too hard to prove a point, Satan tempts us to either betray a confidence or restructure the truth a little. Ground is lost which may never be regained.

> Set a guard over my mouth, O LORD; keep watch
> over the door of my lips (Psalm 141:3).

Not addicted to wine. Not only does Titus 2 teach discretion in what comes out of our mouths, it also teaches moderation in what goes in. Although Paul addresses a specific area, I believe our lifestyle should also reflect stability and moderation. Everything from our calorie intake to our shopping mall excursions fall within the shadow of these words in Titus. Because God never commends impulsiveness as a way of life, you and I must cultivate self-control.

Able to teach what is good. A look at the detailed notes Paul wrote Timothy gives us some insight about "what is good."

> And is well known for her good deeds, such as bringing up children, showing hospitality, washing the feet of the saints, helping those in trouble and devoting herself to all kinds of good deeds (1 Timothy 5:10).

The New English Bible translation of the last phrase gives the idea that this woman has taken every opportunity of doing good.

Living an inconspicuously good life apparently won't do it! We older women should have a *reputation* for our kindnesses to others. I hear Paul saying in this passage that our character and lifestyle must glow with a godly goodness which is easily documented by everyone whose lives we touch. Our parenting, our hospitality, our concern for God's hurting people, our willingness to serve, and how quickly we reach out to all kinds of people are all a part of the good we do.

My dictionary offers further insights into the meaning of *good.* It explains that the good we women are to teach would be something that: possesses desirable qualities; promotes success, welfare, happiness, or is otherwise beneficial and satisfying; is fitting, appropriate, advantageous, full; is genuine, not counterfeit; is true, valid, virtuous, pure, not shabby or worn.

God tells us throughout the Bible to be good . . . to love and to teach what is good. . . to cling to and be ready to do what is good. I believe the Lord expects you and me to study out His definition of *good.* Is a "do-gooder" different than someone teaching good and being good? Beware the well-camouflaged selfishness that motivates some "doing good." When I display apparent generosity or unselfishness on my terms, I'm into the wrong kind of good deeds; I'm in trouble.

Who Can Mentor?

Titus 2 details an ambitious job description, but a woman with those qualities—or one who is growing toward them—could put life on fast-forward for the younger women in her sphere of influence!

OTHER IMPORTANT QUALITIES

In addition to what we find in Titus 2, I've listed here some other important qualities for mentors. I believe they will be true of women who take God seriously.

Being available and willing to share in another's life. Jesus Christ gave quality time and attention to His followers. He chose the disciples to "be with him" (Mark 3:14). He knew what parents always discover about raising children: The most effective teaching comes through example. It's impossible to make either apostles or godly children by proxy.

Jesus unconditionally shared His life with the Twelve. The disciples fished with Jesus, journeyed and ate with Him, talked with and questioned Him, prayed with Him, and celebrated the Passover with Him. As they shared intimately in Christ's life, they gradually absorbed His priorities, His ministry secrets, and His absolute obedience to the Father's will.

The superficial greeting or the last three minutes before another appointment was never Jesus' style. Jesus gifted those He discipled with attention, love, and training.

Longing to know God better. Jesus' disciples longed to know Him more intimately. Actually, the word *disciple* translates into "learner, apprentice, follower." God always reveals Himself to those who seek Him.

In the process of becoming godly women, we need to long to know our sovereign God intimately. This longing comes through knowing the Word, God's love letter and rule book for His children. It also comes through remembering what Jesus is like and loving what He does.

You and I need to abide in Christ. *Abiding* means that we are permanently a part of Christ—all of the way, all of the time. We don't willfully plug in or out based on whim or feeling. We should be growing in our awareness of Him.

Desiring to listen with a receptive heart. Younger women need role models who can listen with an accepting rather than a judging attitude; women who can listen without thinking, *As soon as she pauses, I'll say . . .* They need listeners who hear not only the facts, but also the meanings and the feelings behind those facts; who refrain from unnecessary questions or promptings. As David Augsburger put it in *Caring Enough to Confront*, "I want to hear you, and not hear myself interpreting you."

Understanding the commitment needed in disciplemaking and persevering as disciplers. Commitment means keeping on keeping on—even when the initial "shine" of a project (or a discipling relationship) wears thin.

I don't believe, however, that God expects us to bury our brains when we commit ourselves to follow His precepts. We need to understand our limits and capabilities before we can know the appropriate extent of a first mentoring relationship. We need to ask the Holy Spirit to clearly show us—a step at a time—the long-range boundaries of our nurturing activities.

Being willing to spiritually reproduce herself, nurturing new disciples who will eventually become disciplemakers themselves. "And the things you have heard me say in the presence of many witnesses entrust to reliable [women] who will also be qualified to teach others" (2 Timothy 2:2). It sounds as if Paul is talking about disciplemaking! When some younger women include as a personal goal this idea of reproducing themselves, I rejoice. And I suspect that God rejoices too.

FACING UP TO UNCERTAINTIES

Experience has taught me that older women often feel threatened by younger ones. And young women feel intimidated by the older generation—but for different reasons! We may secretly envy their fresh beauty and up-to-date style, at the same time they may wish for our experience and confidence.

A new mentor usually takes that first step of faith with some hesitation. I certainly did. But I believe you will discover God's complete trustworthiness for handling whatever comes after an initial decision to nurture younger women.

Let's look candidly at three fears which can be stumbling blocks to a discipling relationship.

Fear #1 *"I'm nobody special. I've never led a Bible study or workshop—and am certainly not the type to proclaim myself a role model or shining example of womanhood."*

God uses women like you and me in His discipling ministry. Whenever God gives one of us a vision of ministry He also enables us to complete it successfully. I'm also sure He wants ordinary women like you and me to carry out the guidelines outlined in Titus 2:3-5.

Superstars have neither the time nor the adaptability to mentor on a sustained basis. They may be able to give inspiring talks and encourage large groups, but only you and I can call a tired mother several times a week to ask, "How is it going with your little ones today? Can I play with them while you get groceries?" We can share from God's Word a just-right promise for her needs this week.

Fear #2 *"Something like this sounds risky—to my privacy and personal breathing space, to my time schedule and other responsibilities. Won't this get out of hand?"*

The Christian life teems with needs and opportunities for risk-taking. Jesus took risks for those He loved and discipled. If we consider ourselves followers of Jesus, we may need to eliminate some activities in order to be free to risk. We may need to rearrange our priorities.

I control the time I spend in discipling relationships by focusing on one woman at a time. I set definite scheduling limits and cutoff dates so that the amount of time we will spend together is clear to both of us.

In only one situation did I sometimes feel pressured to spend more time than I had planned. But in Tina's case the pressure originated with me. I saw the complexity of her problems—and her deep need for intensive discipling and counseling—and I desired to help.

You alone make the choices about how available to be. It helps me to remember that a giving lifestyle always leaves me with more to give and enjoy.

Fear #3 *"I don't know how to mentor or disciple. What on earth will we do when we get together?"*

Good question, one which prompted the writing of this book! Chapters 3, 4, and 5 will give you specific tools for mentoring. More importantly, the Holy Spirit will furnish the moment-by-moment guidance and insight you need. Read on!

Young women benefit immeasurably from the experiences and perspectives of more mature women. Even some of the cooking shortcuts we've learned or the hospitality hints we've tucked away in our memory make the way a little easier and happier for our friends.

OUR RESPONSE TO TITUS 2

God asks each of us to become life-shapers. "For none of us lives to himself alone and none of us dies to himself alone. . . . So, whether we live or die, we belong to the Lord" (Romans 14:7-8).

"I am available to you, Lord." Those words, which brighten the inside of my Bible's cover, remind me of a changepoint time in my spiritual journey—a corner turned on February 27, 1966.

Perhaps you would like to demonstrate to God that *you've* decided to take Him seriously about His Titus 2 imperative. Perhaps you'll want to note today's date alongside your decision. As you do, you may want to pray this prayer, adding whatever additional thoughts your heart suggests.

> Lord, there's a part of me that's afraid to give myself
> to You but the other part longs for this kind of a
> relationship with You. I want to be available to You,

available to others. I trust You to show me who You want me to reach out to. I just want to be available.

MORE WORTHY WOMEN IDEAS

1. Which individuals have modeled excellence for you at different stages of your life? Can you single out the particular ways they influenced you? Have you let them know what this meant to you?

2. Choose either the Titus 2 directive "to be reverent in the way they live" or "to teach what is good" and then list the specific ways you can carry out this precept in your everyday life. What difference could this make for your family? Your friends?

3. Begin a study on what the Bible shows us about *example*. Check out these Scriptures: 1 Peter 2:21-24 (example by imitation), 1 Timothy 4:12 (example of excellence), Titus 2:3-8 (example in teaching and godly life); Hebrews 4:11 (warning for a poor example).

1. Rebecca Manley Pippert, *Out of the Saltshaker* (Downers Grove: InterVarsity Press, 1979), p. 119.

3

HOW DO I GET STARTED?

———————————————————————————————————————

I clearly remember the day I stopped making excuses and decided to disciple Marni.

I was sitting at my desk as my eyes moved to a delicate mobile of angels made of wood shavings and feathers. My mind slid back through more than twenty years, to Kim.

During Kim's shy junior high years I became her prayer pal. I never succeeded in drawing her out in conversation, but she always seemed pleased with my notes and assurances of prayer support. Most of her peers showed more self-confidence as they matured, but Kim remained shy and reclusive.

Her older sister visited me during Christmas vacation, bringing a small gift—the bit of angel fluff. She reported that Kim was too bashful to deliver it in person. I wrote Kim a note of thanks and told her again that I loved her and prayed for her.

But I lost track of my shy young friend—until the day I heard the devastating news. Kim had disappeared without leaving any hint to help those who searched for her, day after week after month after year. No one has heard from her; no clue has surfaced to answer the "what happened?" questions.

That lost opportunity still disturbs me. Instead of remaining in my personal comfort zone, why didn't I make the effort to find out what the inside of Kim was like?

I wasn't going to make the same mistake with Marni!

I've learned that when the Holy Spirit brings someone to mind, we need to respond. And it's important that we do it *now*.

Perhaps the last chapter helped you discover that God's role model requirements aren't difficult. You see they're attainable and have faced up to uncertainties which could inhibit your becoming a Titus 2 woman. You also understand the deep longing many women have to be mentored and you have a clearer picture of the special needs for mentoring.

Perhaps the Holy Spirit has whispered to you words like, "This ministry is something *you* could grow into comfortably. And it would satisfy your urge to see certain values built into God's women from generation to generation. Go for it!"

But perhaps you're uncertain about how to begin. Maybe you've received no phone call or note or in-person query asking you to spend regular time with a younger Christian. Should you initiate the discipling? I've found an enthusiastic "yes" answers that question!

HOW DO I FIND SOMEONE TO DISCIPLE?

I've learned that some young women will never ask for help—even when they're your friends. Unless you and I are looking for their silent pleas, we may be unaware that they would welcome a mentoring relationship. Be willing to seek out these women with the guidance of the Holy Spirit. At times I've said: "How about our getting together for an hour or so each week—for some Bible study and talking together?" Practice alerting yourself to the younger woman's plea for nurture, whether she expresses this directly or indirectly. Sensitivity to other women's feelings—having your "antenna" up—makes the difference.

Many of my nurturing relationships have begun naturally. A discipling relationship grew out of the five years of warm friendship Shelley and I had enjoyed. We were celebrating her birthday with lunch together when the discussion turned abruptly. Shelley asked if we could start getting together weekly in order to get her priorities in line and to study the Word.

At other times my heart has touched the heart of another woman as we talked after a church potluck or worked together in Kids' Klub. I've found that opportunities are plentiful for the woman whose heart and eyes are open.

Once I've sensed that a woman wants a mentor, I look for other qualities which I feel are essential for an effective relationship. Here's a list of questions I find helpful as I prayerfully consider the possibility of a closer relationship:

Do we enjoy each other? Is this person comfortable with me? Am I comfortable with her?

Is this woman open to learning? Does she have a searching and questioning attitude?

Is she willing to commit to our meeting together and to do the assignments and projects I might suggest? Commitment is sometimes lacking in many who grew up in the fifties and sixties.

THINKING THROUGH THE FIRST MEETING

Janet sounded worried. "Now that Sandy and I have decided to get together regularly, what do I *do*?"

I suggested that she might want to use my three checkpoints to prepare herself for a first meeting.

41

How Do I Get Started?

1. *Set up a time to meet.* Initially I like to take my new friend out to lunch—to a quiet place where we can talk easily. Meeting on neutral ground helps in the move from a casual friendship to a discipling relationship.

2. *Ask your potential disciple to bring her written goals to your first meeting.* These should reflect her personal needs, as well as what she wants or expects from the mentoring relationship. In this way you can minister to her more effectively. I believe it becomes too easy to superficially focus on someone's apparent needs. Real and felt needs surface in even the briefest written objectives.

3. *List your goals for the relationship.* I often share these with the women I disciple. Some examples of the goals I may write are:

> I see a great need to help Shelley build a self-esteem which is based on God's precepts rather than on the negative feedback she gets from Jim.

> I want Stephanie to trust me and relate to me in a way she hasn't allowed herself before. I want to help her learn vulnerability's healing—while I learn alongside her.

GETTING TO KNOW EACH OTHER

During the first discipling time, you want to:

1. *Decide when and how often to get together.* Be sure to set an approximate cutoff date. Even if this needs adjusting later, you both need a clear-cut time limit. As you take into consideration your own family needs and schedule, you might suggest two or three possible times.

I suggest meeting for anywhere between ten and eighteen times over a period of three to nine months. Each meeting should range from one and one-half to two and one-half hours of uninterrupted time. Your schedules will determine whether those hours are spent in the morning, afternoon, or evening.

2. *Emphasize your commitment to this schedule and ask for her commitment.* I tell my friend that I believe we both would be losers if either of us failed to keep our commitment to those prearranged meetings. Sometimes illness or family needs make a postponement necessary, but sticking to the previously arranged dates and times whenever possible works better for both women. The world already has too many no-shows.

3. *Discuss her goals.* Some of the questions we talk through include these on goalsetting:

> Are your goals expressed clearly?
> What is the motivation behind each goal?
> Are your goals realistic?
> How will you measure your progress in each?

Although I take home my friend's list (it will serve as a key planning tool for me), I make sure she also keeps a copy. She needs to check on her progress, perhaps even more closely than I do. Sometimes I've noticed that the objectives have been accomplished without much special attention—almost as a by-product of the disciplemaking process.

Throughout this book you will see how these goals are used to prepare for effective mentoring, but in Chapters 4 and 5 we talk specifically about accountability and goals.

4. *Discuss the kind of study to have and consider books you might use in addition to the Bible.* I've used Bible study workbooks a few times, but have felt disappointed for the most part. A fill-in-the-blanks study seems to inhibit spontaneity and warmth. I also think some individuals have negative feelings toward workbooks in general—often stemming from the Sunday school workbooks of their childhood.

Here are some topics for study:

> the worthy woman characteristics in Proverbs 31:10-30
>
> Ruth's character qualities (book of Ruth)
>
> the ways Naomi helped Ruth to become a godly
> woman (book of Ruth)

How Do I Get Started?

Titus 2:3-5

I often compile a study based on my disciple's goals.

Appropriate topics abound. Some appear within this book, but you will find additional suggestions in Appendix A, followed by material on biblical women in Appendix B.

THINKING THROUGH LOCATION AND LOGISTICS

After our first meeting, I usually ask my friend to come to my home. If this is possible for you, I encourage you to do the same. Your home is your natural environment, an extension of your personality. The one receiving your mentoring should see what kind of "keeper at home" you are.

When a young woman comes to my home she can enjoy the old family furnishings (some antique and some early-married) and the growing number of framed grandchildren. When she looks at our dining room wall she sees the pictures of missionary and international friends we have communicated with during the last twenty-five years. Without my saying anything I have disclosed to her what I value.

Since we usually want a time and place of uninterrupted quiet, I sometimes disconnect the telephone. But I never totally shut out or ignore family members, except when confidentiality would be threatened. My family is also an extension of me.

If you have young children at home, it may take creativity to settle on a mutually satisfactory time and place. If discipling had been part of my early married years, I definitely couldn't have done it in my home. I would have settled for less "extension of me" and more uninterrupted moments! It may be more realistic to meet in her home or at a restaurant.

One of my friends in this youngsters-at-home stage limits her discipling times to evenings—8:00 to 9:30 P.M.—when her husband can shortstop any extra drinks of water and other bedtime crises that could play havoc with the time. Another young mother has a standing arrangement for Grandma to host the youngsters every Tuesday afternoon.

DON'T DELAY

I'm a slow starter—whether I'm initiating a new writing project or getting out of bed in the morning. I've procrastinated work on this chapter by carefully (and needlessly) rearranging my notes, then brewing a mug of hot tea. Even as I write these words, my mind looks out the window and flirts with the idea of checking the barometer in the next room. Like the cartoon over my sink says, I'm a slow starter . . . all day!

Don't delay the blessings of nurturing other women. Do it your way, but—most importantly—do it now!

MORE WORTHY WOMAN IDEAS

1. What two options might be open for giving you and your younger friend quiet and uninterrupted times together? What times and days of the week would work best for you?

2. What areas of your life have you rationalized about or lacked discipline in? Tackle a specific one now and record your progress.

3. Select one of the gospels and note for yourself the character qualities Jesus demonstrated. Which seems most important for *your* Christian growth? Why?

4

IS THERE A RECIPE FOR DISCIPLING TIMES?

"Guess what happened?" Marni called as she rushed through our gate on that velvety-crisp September morning. As she settled in beside me on the porch, her voice bubbled with a hint of laughter. "Well, Sam set the alarm for 6:00 this morning so he could go to the men's Bible study. That's really a milestone for my husband because he is not a morning person."

I started to reply, but Marni's story wasn't finished. "I was awake enough to see Sam scrunched over the edge of the bed, putting on his shoes and muttering something about leaving at such a ridiculously early hour.

"Trying to encourage him, I said, 'Well, Honey, I'm sure your getting up and going to Bible study pleases God.'

"After a few seconds of absolute silence, Sam grumbled, 'I'll bet God isn't even up yet.'"

Laughing together, Marni and I plunged into another session of nurturing and two-way learning.

THE INGREDIENTS OF OUR TOGETHER-TIMES

How does one prepare for these sessions? Let me tell you what has been invaluable to me: I prepare a lesson plan each week. As I think and pray through our time together, I'm aware that my plan is not absolute—there will be times when I may have to abandon it to meet an urgent need.

Each plan covers the same particulars, whether I'm meeting with a small group or with just one woman. They are:

> Praise and worship
> Encouragement and prayer
> Accountability and checking progress on goals
> Study which focuses on God's insights for
>   Christian maturity
> Assignments

I change the order from time to time to prevent the feeling of conforming to a formula. And since prayer, encouragement, and worship are closely aligned, the segments overlap and flow into one another easily.

PRAISE AND WORSHIP

I've found that praise sets the tone for our time together. It causes us to focus on who God is and what He has done. "Praise is a matter of life and breath. That is, praise must come from a genuine and vital relationship with God, and praise must be vocal . . . not silent."[1]

These moments also model a mindset that Christian women need to develop. Under your example and with your guidance, your friend can learn how to praise God.

Before our session I use both my Bible and hymnal in planning our praise time. Study books such as a concordance, commentary, and Bible handbook help me in choosing appropriate passages in the Word. (Additional study books are listed in Appendix A.)

As I prayerfully select a passage of Scripture, I consciously keep in mind our topic of study and my friend's needs and goals. For example, after Marni's struggle with anger surfaced, some of the Scriptures I selected focused on God's perspective of this sometimes unwieldy emotion. One that we shared was Galatians 5:22-23: "But the fruit of the Spirit is love, joy, peace, patience, kindness, goodness, faithfulness, gentleness, and self-control. Against such things there is no law."

Of the many inspiring Scripture passages to meditate on and rejoice in, I might select from sections such as these:

- 1 Samuel 2:1-10 discloses Hannah's beautiful prayer after she gave her much-loved son Samuel to the Lord. It includes the words, "There is no one holy like the LORD; there is no one besides you; there is no Rock like our God."

- Ephesians 3:14-21 begins with the powerful prayer of Paul, "For this reason I kneel before the Father, from whom his whole family in heaven and on earth derives its name. I pray that out of his glorious riches he may strengthen you with power through his Spirit in your inner being, so that Christ may dwell in your hearts through faith."

- 1 Chronicles 29:10-19 repeats David's praises before the assembly of people who had given freely to the Lord's work of temple-building, before Solomon was made king. In the midst of that section we read, "But who am I, and who are my people, that we should be able to give as generously as this?

> Everything comes from you, and we have given you only what comes from your hand."

- Luke 1:46-55 gives us Mary's radiant song: "My soul [praises] the Lord and my spirit rejoices in God my Savior."

- Romans 8:35-39 asks "Who shall separate us from the love of Christ? Shall trouble or hardship or persecution or famine or nakedness or danger or sword? . . . Neither the present nor the future, nor any powers, neither height nor depth, nor anything else in all creation, will be able to separate us from the love of God that is in Christ Jesus our Lord."

- The Psalms offer unlimited worship and praise thoughts—try chapters 16, 46, 73, 90, 121, 136, 139, 145. .

- Isaiah's words also provide many worship-flavored sections to read aloud: chapters 40:9-11; 21-31; 43:1-2, 18-19; and 55.

- Jabez's prayer in 1 Chronicles 4:10.

I also explore various ways of meditating on the Scripture presented each week. Here are some ideas you may want to adapt:

- Read the verses in unison one week, then read responsively another time.

- Memorize a verse together.

- Try paraphrasing on paper some verses of a psalm, or personalizing that paraphrase with your own name before sharing it aloud.

For example:

> How long, O LORD? Will you forget me forever?
> How long will you hide your face from me?
> How long must I wrestle with my thoughts and
>   every day have sorrow in my heart?
> How long will my enemy triumph over me?

Look on me and answer, O LORD my God.
Give light to my eyes, or I will sleep in death;
my enemy will say, "I have overcome him,"
  and my foes will rejoice when I fall.
But I trust in your unfailing love;
my heart rejoices in your salvation.
I will sing to the LORD, for he has been good to me.
                                            Psalm 13

Shelley's paraphrase read:

> Sometimes, Lord, it seems like the ungodly—the
> non-Christians—have all the breaks, and I feel im-
> posed upon and a little frightened. Then it is that
> I am overwhelmed with the knowledge that your
> mercy and love toward me is forever. The ungodly
> have so little time to enjoy their small pleasures. So
> my grumbling lament turns into a song of praise
> to such a wonderful Lord!

Sometimes we focus on a topic, such as:

- God's incredible creation
- His character qualities (faithfulness, love, holiness, power, etc.)
- the names given to God in Scripture—included are:

> Elohim (the mighty creator; strong, mighty, prominent, committed to His people)
>   Genesis 1
> Adonai (the Lord of my life)
>   Genesis 15:1-8
> El Shaddai (sufficient for all my needs)
>   Genesis 17:1, John 15
> Jehovah (the Redeemer, the always present, self-existent one)
>   Exodus 3:14-15
> Abba (a Father to the fatherless)
>   Psalm 68:5-6, Matthew 6:9

Some study Bibles (right now I'm looking at *The Open Bible*) give extensive lists of names of God, along with Scripture references. Bible handbooks are another source for the names of God in Scripture.

As you discuss your thoughts and applications, your friend will develop confidence to make these same discoveries in Scripture on her own. After you've established a good rapport, ask her to lead your praise time from time to time. Assure her of your help in getting started.

ENCOURAGEMENT AND PRAYER

I usually spend about ten minutes in praise and then make the transition into sharing and praying.

One of the most powerful parts of nurturing comes in praying. The mentor may do most of the praying, especially at first, but God works strongly during these times of prayer.

Remember Jesus' willingness to be vulnerable? God uses role models who are transparent. We need to tell others of the sore places within our hearts as well as the joys. When I've told what God is doing in my life, and what I want Him to do, it becomes easier for others to do the same. Asking for support—and admitting our hurts and hurdles—will affirm our desire to become a better wife or roommate or mother. I've asked for prayer about: starting a neighborhood Bible study, terminating an uncomfortable community responsibility, needed attitude changes, my husband's impending job changes, financial struggles, and hassles with my ailing refrigerator.

Each time we are together I ask, "How can I most effectively pray for you this week?" I write down those requests so that I will be praying on a daily basis. This list serves as a tool for follow-up and accountability as well.

This two-way vulnerability helps our partners grasp how much we need their prayers, and helps both of us as we pray specifically for each other during the week.

One word of caution: never pressure your partner into praying. I remember one young woman desired "to express my struggles so others can pray for my problem areas; to not feel afraid to open myself up." Praying aloud seems terribly intimidating to someone who has never done so. Just the sound of one's own voice can detonate shock waves!

As you encourage your friend to eventually pray aloud— for your needs and hers—talk about conversational prayer. By conversational prayer I mean praying spontaneously, using one or two sentences, and with no particular order. The prayer of one may trigger an affirming sentence or two of additional prayer by the other so that we build on one another's thoughts.

Practice using this comfortable, refreshing method of prayer so she won't hang back in fear of not sounding "spiritual enough." I have to constantly check myself to make certain my prayers remain simple, pointed, and short.

My father long ago quoted to me a traditional prayer used by fishermen on the coast of France: "O God, thy sea is so great and my boat is so small!" For a long time I thought this hardly qualified as a prayer, yet now I see that these terse words contain the essence of all prayer: an acknowledgment of God's power.

ACCOUNTABILITY AND GOALS

Because goals are covered in the next chapter, we will move on to accountability's place in the discipling recipe.

I've always responded more positively to a teacher or role model who expects quite a bit of me, rather than one who lets me "get by." Somehow I rise to the challenge.

Karen Burton Mains writes:

When David and I were still in the pastorate, I started a number of "growth groups" among the women in our church for the purpose of accelerating spiritual growth. These groups met for two months and had no more than six members.

Each person named the areas in which she needed to grow, and then asked the group for help. . . .

> Accountability always works like a charm. If I know
> someone is going to phone me at a certain time, it
> gives me tremendous impetus to do what I know I
> need to do!"[2]

Luke 12:48 says "From everyone who has been given much,
much will be demanded." Don't these words also suggest the
responsibility you and I carry for those we disciple and for
what we ask of them?

Eva asked me recently, "What if your disciple repeatedly
fails to follow through, even though she always comes, listens,
and seems to want to learn?"

I'm still learning how to answer this stickler. After a reasonable time period with no signs of follow-through (perhaps
three to five weeks), I suspect that we must confront the
younger woman in some way. This is biblical.

By nature I'm always loathe to confront anyone, but I've
come to realize that both of us waste our time without evident
life changes showing. My discipling friend needs to hear direct
and insistent questions from me, like, "How serious are you
about making these changes?" and "What step did you take
yesterday toward your goal of . . .?"

If nothing happens for six to eight weeks, you have two
options: 1. terminate the relationship after fully explaining
the roadblock or 2. continue as though the young woman *is*
following through, reminding yourself that God may be doing
more in her life than you can discern right now.

Within the discipling relationship, accountability is a natural follow-up to goals and concerns. Asked in the context of
love, accountability questions don't sound threatening.

"How did that telephone call turn out?"

"Did you swim ten laps yesterday?"

"Caryn, let me hear that section of Romans you worked
on last week."

As grateful as I am for God's grace, I also appreciate a

Heavenly Father who demands accountability. On our own, you and I become incredibly skilled at rationalizing and avoiding the risk that goes with vulnerability within a relationship. Beth Mainhood writes:

> A protective spiritual umbrella—a person or a group who holds us accountable, encourages us, and challenges us—is spiritually vital. When we help others, we become a part of the protection they need. We, too, need that kind of interpersonal protection."[3]

STUDY FOR CHRISTIAN MATURITY

Even though my experience has been that a highly structured Bible study isn't what we want in this warm relationship, we certainly study and use the Word. It remains foundational.

God never wastes time given to Him. With a good concordance and my Bible in front of me, I spend time searching out appropriate Scripture. From the time I put into the preparation I always draw out valuable nourishment for my inner woman.

As I've talked with women about their preparation for the study time, I frequently hear two questions: How can I be sure our study meets my friend's needs? How much time should we spend on this topic?

How can I be sure our study meets my friend's needs? In studying the Bible with younger women, I've discovered the importance of knowing well both the Word and the woman I'm mentoring. I try to make our study applicable to her situation—her struggles or desires or relationships or circumstances. Every time we meet I ask the Holy Spirit to lead and reveal Christ to both of us.

For example, when Marni disclosed that anger was a growing problem in her life, we not only focused on God's perspective during our praise and worship time, we also studied what the Bible says about anger. In addition, I asked her to read some books.[4]

Is There a Recipe for Discipling Times?

Marni and I studied Bible passages such as these:

2 Timothy 1:7—"For God did not give us a spirit of timidity, but a spirit of power, of love and of self-discipline."

James 1:19-20—"My dear [sisters], take note of this: Everyone should be quick to listen, slow to speak and slow to become angry, for [a woman's] anger does not bring about the righteous life that God desires."

Proverbs 19:11—"A [woman's] wisdom gives [her] patience; it is to [her] glory to overlook an offense."

1 Peter 3:3-4—"Your beauty should not come from outward adornment. . . . Instead, it should be that of your inner self, the unfading beauty of a gentle and quiet spirit, which is of great worth in God's sight."

How much time should I spend on a topic? Certain circumstances—such as the complexity and depth of a need—might prompt spending almost all of our time on one topic. However, up to now, my own experience has shown that even women with unsettling problems need an introduction to a variety and breadth of topics. They also need the total mentoring and discipling recipe we've looked at here.

Sometimes more than one session is needed to adequately cover a topic before moving on to the next. For example, Marni and I spent three weeks discussing anger. Time frames may get pushed aside when spontaneous discussion or extra-curricular activities prolong our study. I've found that the Holy Spirit will help me discern when it's time to move on.

You and I need to model the importance of being on time and following through on commitments. We must teach both responsibility and flexibility.

ASSIGNMENTS BRIDGE THE BETWEEN-TIMES

Never conclude without discussing what God's Word and other credible sources say.

At the conclusion of our time together, I usually give specific homework assignments. I do this for several reasons. First, it fills in the time gap between our face-to-face meetings, keeping us daily and consistently focused on our current subject. Homework also provides built-in responsibility and accountability. It lets me know how seriously my friend wants to grow; how effectively my time is being used.

And she needs this chance to translate into everyday life what she is learning. For example, I suggested that Marni:

Ask her husband's help, understanding, and prayers.

Set up a tape recorder, for later listening and evaluating what she heard. Did she notice a habit or pattern?

Postpone her outbursts for sixty seconds, allowing time for reconsideration and cooling down.

Refrain from taking the responsibility for someone else's behavior, realizing that someone else's belief isn't necessarily hers.

Sometimes I ask my discipling partner to choose five suggestions (from our discussion and Scripture, or perhaps from a book I've loaned her), then to try them before sharing the results with me later. I try to mix practical application assignments with study assignments. A list of additional examples of homework is included in Appendix C.

In order to help motivate my disciple, I often telephone midweek to ask how she's doing. Don't all of us respond best to whatever someone else both expects and inspects? Occasionally I write out a favorite quotation to send home as extra support that week. But always the assignment fits the disciple and where she is "living" at the moment.

Immediately after each session I've found it very helpful to make notes on our discussion. I include the other woman's responses and needs—anything that will help me as I mentor and nurture. Then I re-read those notes just before we get together again.

BECOMING GOD'S KIND OF WOMAN

These informally structured meetings in my home, with young women like Marni, seem to fit my temperament and make maximum use of the spiritual gifts God expects me to use. This one-on-one style of discipling has proved to be effective and gratifying.

In some ways mentors resemble resource material. But instead of sitting on a library shelf, we are found in our individual spheres of influence—our homes and offices and churches. Just as a good library boasts volumes of all sizes and colors and content, God effectively uses the different personalities and experiences of mentors.

The kind of women you and I really are, all by ourselves before God, carries a weightier value than a thoroughly prepared lesson. But don't allow this truth to lead you astray. I've found that preparation—in prayer and in mapping out our time together—makes a tremendous difference in how I feel about disciplemaking and whether or not my efforts are effective.

The balance of ingredients in my favorite muffin recipe is crucial. Too much or too little baking powder spells out a culinary disaster; a forgotten ingredient can cancel everything I've already put in. For nurturing, the recipe becomes equally important.

MORE WORTHY WOMAN IDEAS

1. Follow Shelley's example and write a "praise note" to your Lord.
2. Select one or more of the homework assignments from the previous pages or in the appendix and complete them within the next month.
3. What other names of God (in addition to the ones given on page 51) can you find in Scripture? Write down the reference and meaning.

1. Ronald B. Allen, *Praise! A Matter of Life and Breath* (Nashville: Thomas Nelson Publishers, 1980), p. 58.

2. Karen Burton Mains, "Warming Up," *Sunday Digest* January 13, 1985, p. 4.

3. Beth Mainhood, *Reaching Your World: Disciplemaking for Women,* (Colorado Springs: NavPress, 1986), pp. 35-36.

4. Resource books dealing with anger:

- James Dobson, *Emotions: Can You Trust Them?* (Regal Books, 1980).
- Paul A. Hauck, *Overcoming Frustration and Anger* (Westminster Press, 1974).
- Erwin W. Lutzer, *How To Say No To a Stubborn Habit* (Victor Books, 1979).
- Erwin W. Lutzer, *Managing Your Emotions* (Victor Books, 1983).
- Charles Swindoll, *Anger* (booklet) (Multnomah Press, 1980).

5

HOW DO WE USE
GOALS IN DISCIPLING?

—————————————————————

"Not having a goal is more to be feared than not reaching a goal. . . . I would rather attempt to do something great and fail, than attempt to do nothing and succeed." Victor Frankl's words have challenged me to attempt some things I've not wanted to risk in the past.

For me, joining an aerobics exercise class at our church seemed an incredibly threatening experience. Only another older, out-of-shape woman would understand the stress I felt each time I walked in to start those strenuous routines.

How Do We Use Goals in Discipling?

The workout demanded 125 percent of my available energy, but I felt even more devastated by so many slim, youthful bodies around me. In the midst of those high-fashion leotards, my baggy gray warm-up pants obviously weren't going to make the pages of *Today's Christian Woman*. And what the instructor termed a "healthy glow" on those other bodies amounted to sweat and heavy breathing on mine.

Moving from the comfortable niche of a role model to the bottom of the fitness heap quickly tumbled any prideful attitudes elbowing for a place in my mind.

My discipleship partners held me accountable to my goal and encouraged me along the way. I wouldn't have stayed in the program without them!

WRITING OUT SPECIFIC GOALS

Approximately a third of the way through the scheduled number of discipling gatherings, I focus on goals. We've talked about them before, but now the time has come to turn that "grocery list" of hopes and dreams into something tangible the young woman can work with and grow with—long after we have ceased meeting together.

At this time we begin to fill out a goal chart which will be used in our remaining time together. Perhaps the different categories (spiritual, financial, etc.) will be sketchy at first, but at least one goal in each category should be noted and implemented from a daily to long-term basis. Each goal should be measurable and attainable.

As I look at these needs and specific areas of the younger woman's life, my job is to challenge her in ways she may not have initially considered. By now I'm more aware of my disciple's values and background and potential. My notes on these matters enable me to focus more clearly on the areas she needs to be encouraged to grow in.

So that you can see an example of one way to chart goals, I'm including Mary Jo's chart, "Goal Setting for A Better You," on the next page. You may want to adapt this form for your

Goal Setting . . . For a Better You

	Daily Goals	Short-term Goals	Long-term Goals
Physical	Exercise 30-40 minutes Eliminate "junk" foods	Start bike riding on Saturday with husband Walk instead of always using car; increase walking pace	Cut down on frequent colds and flu In shape for biking along coast
Financial	Eliminate impulse buying; use lists regularly Fix lunches to go more often	Set up monthly budget system; use it. Use less expensive ingredients in meals	Discover a way to earn money at home; save 50% of this for furnishing new house Save enough for vacation to Canada
Mental	Read to keep current with news Learn new word and use it	Focus on political situation and economy in one country Use library card regularly	Take a typing or speed reading course Start on-going journal
Spiritual	Start Daily Walk plan for reading through the Bible. Begin a prayer list; write out prayers sometimes Hum praise chorus whenever my mind starts on a downward cycle; think "content" thoughts	Read at least one Christian book and one Christian magazine monthly Begin to memorize Scripture (sections I've marked from discipling) Focus on God's sovereignty by studying in the Word	Encourage husband to lead a home Bible study or care group Meet regularly with younger woman for six months, in discipling situation Make inner peace and stability a lifestyle
Home and family	Use time chart just made	Be creative in hospitality; sensitive to needs of others. (Invite someone new to dinner) Try a new food or recipe, and use in a new menu combination soon	Planned hospitality, to include old and new friends - two or three times/month Complete three needlework projects to have on hand for gifts
Personal	Plan ½ hour for myself; fun project or just goofing off Write or phone a friend	Work on different aspects of myself each month (e.g. self-image, communication, interpersonal relationships, poise) Plan to have lunch or coffee break with friend I've lost track of	Learn to fix hair and makeup in newer, more becoming ways Try something I'd never thought I could do . . . because I probably can

63

own use. Individual lifestyles and needs affect both the categories and time range of the goals each woman sets.

Once you discover your personal priorities you'll find it easier to shape your goals. For example, in order to complete my longer-range goal of finishing this book, I needed to carefully budget the time needed for the job, planning daily targets for sections completed as well as monthly ones. And Mary Jo had to faithfully follow through on her daily goals of exercise and diet in order to achieve the physical condition needed for the coast bike trip.

HELPING MARY JO ACHIEVE HER GOALS

Because I'm basically a practical person and I suspect that many of you are too, what follows is a "walk" through my actual preparations and meetings with Mary Jo. We'll focus on four of her goals.

On my study wall at home, I posted her want list.

1. Time alone with God. I need a more systematic Bible study—and why don't I pray more naturally?
2. A more disciplined lifestyle—less impulse, more planning.
3. Feel better about myself, less self-conscious.
4. How to develop inner peace in the midst of life's storms —more steadiness, and fewer highs and lows.

I reminded myself that I couldn't set any goals for Mary Jo, but wrote out what I might do to help her make certain changes in her life:

1. Use praise and worship times to familiarize Mary Jo with a committed prayer life.
2. Help her track down her current time expenditures.
3. Could I use the Book of Ruth and Proverbs 31 to help boost Mary Jo's feelings of self-worth? Also use examples of women we both know.

4. Work through the concept of God's sovereignty with her.

Looking at both lists, I mentally and prayerfully cleared the way for helping with those specific needs.

#1 - TIME ALONE WITH GOD

As I thought about how to help Mary Jo reach this goal, I remembered my own undisciplined devotional times when I was also a new Christian and just about Mary Jo's age. Because I recalled feeling overwhelmed by the challenge of living the Christian life, I wanted to break each of her goals into smaller steps. For example, I suggested she learn Scripture that spoke to *her* needs and heart. I recommended she do this while exercising or walking to the store.

Through our weekly moments of praise and worship, Mary Jo began to spot creative ideas to improve her own devotional times with God. When we talked about prayer habits, we discussed the need to quiet our minds before God, to eliminate distractions.

One of us found this centuries-old thought:

Let us thus quiet all the movements of our hearts, as soon as we see them agitated. . . . At the sight of God's majesty, our spirit should become calm and remain serene. One word of the Lord's once immediately calmed a wildly raging sea. One glance of him toward us and of us toward him, should even now do the same thing.[1]

I also encouraged Mary Jo to write out her prayers. The silence she was learning to treasure added zest and meaning to her prayer life. She let me read this brief prayer:

Lord, may I breathe out, following the breathing in I do during worship and Bible study and talking to you. I want others to know I've been touched by the sweet breath of your Spirit—especially my sister Jean Ann.

How Do We Use Goals in Discipling?

One day Mary Jo and I focused on the powerful John 15 words about remaining in Christ, the true Vine. To illustrate this truth I told her that as a grandmother many times over, I've often seen the little ones beg to be picked up and held. But just as their wiggly bodies snuggle briefly into my arms, they slither from my lap and run off to a newer attraction. I confessed that often I'm like that impatient child, staying only briefly in my Heavenly Father's strong and eternal arms. Too soon I'm off and dashing about again.

Mary Jo and I saw that obedience and prayer go hand in hand with an abiding-in-Christ lifestyle. My young friend's hunger for a deeper prayer life was both satisfied and intensified in the weeks and years that followed.

She chose the Daily Walk[2] plan for reading through the Bible in a year. She and her husband decided to study in the Word through this program, and enjoyed discussing their findings and questions.

However, if your disciple has young children she will probably select a Bible reading plan that requires less reading and intense concentration. Young mothers seldom have the luxury of sharing quiet Bible study moments with their husbands, as Mary Jo did.

#2 - DISCIPLINE IN DAY-BY-DAY LIVING

To help Mary Jo reach this goal, I decided to encourage her to use some disciplines of time management: time charts, calendars, and a notebook.

Time Charts. We discussed good stewardship of time and money as a part of a more disciplined life. Both of us kept time records for a week (one aspect of "numbering our days. . . to gain a heart of wisdom" Psalm 90:12), then evaluated the expenditure of our hours and minutes. The tyranny of the urgent devastates even well-intentioned schedules.

I then suggested that Mary Jo chart out a plan on how to spend her time. (Her plan appears on the next page.) This would allow her to keep within reasonable time boundaries,

Mary Jo's Schedule for March

	SUNDAY	MONDAY	TUESDAY	WEDNESDAY	THURSDAY	FRIDAY	SATURDAY
7-8:30 A.M.	Quiet time Breakfast Lunch prep	Jog Quiet time Breakfast	Exercise Quiet Time Breakfast	Jog Quiet time Breakfast	Exercise Quiet time Breakfast	Jog Quiet time Breakfast	Breakfast
8:30-9:45 A.M.	Make bed Dress & ready to leave	Tend plants Start SS prep. & study for Wednesday eve.	"Loose time" Clean Bathroom	Review for tonight's Bible study	Tend plants Phone calls? Clean Bathroom	Complete SS prep.	Bike with husband
9:45-Noon	SS & Church	"Loose time"	Wash & iron & mend	Class at Community Center	Discipling two hours	Clean house thoroughly	Clean bath Gardening or inside work together
Lunch	Finish eating & read paper Time with friends or family						
1-3 P.M.		Light cleaning & picking up	Buy week's groceries & other errands Putting food away, etc.	Baking & extra food preparation for week	"Loose time"	Afternoon to goof off	Gardening or painting in bedroom
3-4:30 P.M.		One cupboard or closet cleaned			Letters to family & out-of-town friends		
4:30-6 P.M. Dinner		Start Dinner	Start Dinner	Start Dinner	Start Dinner	Start Dinner	Qt. time & Jrnl. & Personal
Evening	Eve. Church - Snack, reading and talking	Visit Parents or reading	"Catch-up" night or "Loose time"	Home Bible study	TV Reading	Dinner out or friends in	Dinner out or friends in
Odd moments		Work on new curtains & pillows	Special cleaning job	Yard/garden as weather allows	Small repairs	Personal or house projects	

and she could plan ahead more effectively. After seeing where her minutes and hours really went the previous week, Mary Jo could make a fairly realistic time plan.

She found it necessary to include:

Enough time for the routine and necessary activities.

Some time for self, "fenced off" to withstand the plans or jostling of others.

Some "loose time" for others, keeping certain time open to the Lord's opportunities.

Notice that we didn't try to pin Mary Jo down to half-hour segments—too drastic a change for her inner clock! But she could still check herself against the time segments on the chart, to determine how well she was doing. Saturdays feel different for all of us, so I purposely omitted the restricting time categories for that day. Note that in one way or another, Mary Jo's want-to-change list was planned into her weekly schedule.

Women with a job outside the home or with children at home will concoct a very different time schedule. The "givens" for each woman—her needs and special situations—must shape any planning. But don't we all experience greater day by day satisfaction when we feel mostly in charge of our lives, when we control at least the better part of our days and minutes?

Proverbs 16:9 reminded Mary Jo and me that, "In [her] heart a [woman] plans [her] course, but the LORD determines [her] steps." We also needed to admit to the reality of enough hours in every day to do God's perfect will. Discovering his "good and pleasing and perfect will" (Romans 12:2) became our challenge.

Calendars. The second tool I encouraged Mary Jo to use was a calendar. This would help her manage her time on a broader scale. Setting dates—and including different kinds of hospitality in the weeks ahead—helped her reach out to others, as she wanted. She tentatively noted the names of people to ask, and the type of activity: a Saturday brunch or a Sunday evening of popcorn, vegies, and dip after church or an invitation to watch Friday night basketball.

As we discussed Mary Jo's calendar, I told her some learned-along-the-way lessons. My calendar functions best when filled with the activities and people I believe God has in mind for me and my family. I've discovered that the Lord does lead as I practice obedience, but I'm learning not to expect that all these plans will go exactly as anticipated. The goals and plans become my statements of faith, my offerings of myself to God—for Him to use or to change.

Paul's words in Ephesians 5:15-16 get right to the point:

> Live life, then, with a due sense of responsibility, not as [women] who do not know the meaning of life but as those who do. Make the best use of your time, despite all the difficulties of these days (Phillips).

Notebooks. I also encouraged Mary Jo to keep her weekly time plan and monthly calendar in a notebook—a helpful tool for bringing organization to the unorganized. A notebook would keep everything together and could include her goals and notes from our times together.

At times I was tempted to ask if I could check up on her progress by looking at her notebook. But this would have intruded, except for the times she volunteered to show me something she'd written.

My own notebook contains Bible study notes, goals and notations from discipling, "love-notes" to God, and prayer lists. Many women choose to include wardrobe and shopping sections, menus, and a full range of personal helps. (I show this to every woman I meet with—but I never insist that she use one herself.)

Any size notebook will do—most women will choose a standard looseleaf style (about 7 1/2 by 10 inches). The varicolored covers, as well as contents, reflect each woman's unique personality. Mary Jo chose a sunny yellow binding, most appropriate for the cheerful, open person I grew to love dearly.

#3 - BUILD A BETTER SELF-ESTEEM

Mary Jo's third goal needed our attention. We spent two mornings addressing this topic—but with others I've needed more time. Among the young women I know, four out of five accept a poor self-image as a fact of life.

To show you one way of approaching and helping a woman with low self-esteem, I've included most of my lesson plan for one of those two sessions.

Lesson Plan for February 10

Focus:

Self-image
(My task is to teach and model positive precepts of self-worth.)

Praise and Worship:

Psalm 139 (read vs. 1-18, 23-24 aloud, alternately); comment on how this defines my womanhood & hers.

Encouragement and Prayer:

Ask about her parents' visit; about having couple across the street over for Trivial Pursuit; report to her on new Bible study.
Try for conversational praying today.

Accountability and Goals:

Ask Mary Jo to quote the verse she memorized this week.
Ask about her exercise program.

Study:

A. Go back to Psalm 139; ask MJ how she believes God sees her. Read Hebrews 2:6-8, Genesis 1:26-27; stress that she is God's creation. Since God declared what He created good, we need to accept and encourage that thought. He chooses and cherishes.

B. Proverbs 31:10—God's women are rare and valuable,

excellent. Hebrew word means "strength and worth," denotes respect and influence.

C. Ask MJ to name some of God's attributes; how do these affect our self-images? Our identity lies with sovereign Creator.

D. Leviticus 19:18 and Luke 10:25—Feeling good about others depends on respect; balance between self-respect and attitude of servant. Discuss Romans 12:1-3. What God says about us is the point, not how we feel.

Self-respect is only one part of total set of attitudes toward God, others, and self. Depression comes from poor self-esteem. Self-respect is thinking honestly about selves, avoiding extremes, not detracting or deprecating.

E. God valued us enough to send Jesus. Repeat John 3:16 aloud, together. Read and discuss Ephesians 1:3-23—who we are in Christ and what we have in Him.

Assignment:

Read the Book of Ruth and write down her worthy-woman qualities. Do any of these apply to self-image? How? Next time we will review today's discussion and detail Ruth's qualities; will commit to prayer the "action steps" to get MJ moving.

#4 - BALANCE AND PEACE IN MY LIFE

This was the final issue on Mary Jo's list. Throughout our times together we concentrated on this goal.

For beginning moments of worship and praise I incorporated a high percentage of Scripture which dwelt on inner peace and stability. The following verses helped my young friend, but they also reinforced my own need for day by day stability and for greater trust in the Lord.

• Psalm 112:1-8 (steadfast . . . never shaken . . . secure)

- Psalm 1:1-3 (blessed . . . planted)
- Proverbs 13:19-20 (longing fulfilled . . . walks with the wise)
- Ecclesiastes 3:11-13 (eternity in our hearts . . . satisfaction)
- John 14:27 (peace, not as the world gives . . . no fear)
- Romans 8:37-39 (more than conquerors)
- Philippians 4:11-13 (secret of being content . . . through Him)
- 1 Timothy 6:6 (godliness with contentment)
- Hebrews 13:5 (content . . . never left or forsaken)
- Romans 12:9-21 (joyful in hope . . . live at peace)
- Romans 15:1-7, 13 (encouragement, endurance . . . hope)

Along the way it became evident that part of the reason Mary Jo lacked peace was that she had many fears. So for the next couple of weeks, in addition to prayer and some accountability assignments, we looked at Scripture for help in overcoming those fears.

Discovering this kind of unsuspected problem area happens often in a discipling relationship. Sometimes that newly-exposed layer reveals the clue to the most effective mentoring direction to take with a young woman.

When we looked again at the well-balanced life of the worthy woman in Proverbs 31, then pointed out contemporary role models with evident inner peace, Mary Jo saw new glimmers at the end of her tunnel. In studying these women I guided her to see specific character qualities which built in the contentment and inner peace Mary Jo wanted. I helped her keep tabs on the ups and downs of her days and encouraged her with phone calls and visits during stressful periods.

Both of us began to realize how her goals for a better self-image and inner peace were related. As one area began to improve, so did the other. It usually seems to work this way; it always brings a shout of joy to the mentor's heart.

TIPS FOR MOTIVATING

Appropriate motivating always adds impetus to realizing the goals we've set. Mentors need to develop their motivating skills.

My friend Dorothea Fix unknowingly provides the inspiration I need to motivate the women I spend time with. Dorothea knows how to inspire the best in people. She expects it, for one thing. Being married for over thirty-five years to a college track coach probably hasn't detracted from her remarkable talent for motivating others, but my friend initially developed and then honed these skills during thirty-two years of teaching primary students. I'm not surprised that she was one of five finalists for Oregon's Teacher of the Year.

Dorothea sparkles with endless enthusiasm. Her personal warmth and Christlike love for every individual she encounters—from toddlers to senior citizens—breaks through in Dorothea's own words. "My major goal in teaching was to reflect the love of Christ, the joy of my salvation, and my loving concern for these children. Not just while they were my third graders, but in the growing up years ahead."

Dorothea draws heavily on the word *appreciate*. Her applause for the smallest successes of others, and her words of thanks, come quickly and spontaneously. While expecting the best of those she works with, Dorothea also helps people escape the paralysis that comes through fearing failure or through thinking they've blown it for good. She is a motivator and an available listener, a godly woman and a fine role model.

Let this simple acrostic remind you of some basic tips for bringing out the best in others:

A. . . . appreciating and applauding others.

S. . . . studying out their needs.

M. . . . modeling the qualities they seek.

I . . . . imparting enthusiasm as a way of life.

L. . . . listening in a careful and caring way.

E. . . . expecting them to succeed.

How Do We Use Goals in Discipling?

With a smile you are more than halfway there as a mentor!

More Worthy Woman Ideas

1. Set some specific (attainable!) goals for yourself, following some of the suggestions in this chapter. Make a note on your calendar to review your progress at two to three month intervals.

2. Discover and write down examples of good motivators you find in Scripture. What words or events prompt you to include their names?

3. If organizational skills could be the glue in getting and keeping your act together, keep track of your own time expenditures for a week and draw up a time schedule/proposal as Mary Jo did.

1. Francois De La Mothe Fenelon, *Christian Perfection* (New York: Harper and Brothers Publishers, 1947), p. 29.
2. *Daily Walk* (Atlanta: Division of Walk through the Bible Ministries, Inc.)

6

WHAT IS
GOD TEACHING ME
IN TITUS 2?

<hr />

My first discipling effort, over ten years ago, ended in an uneasy failure. Despite the best of intentions, neither Pam nor I knew how to carry out the Titus 2:3-5 precepts. We didn't understand what to expect of one another in the mentoring relationship. And I failed to realize the importance of definite meeting times and accountability. We lacked a specific plan, so our getting together gradually dwindled to almost never.

Pam and I have smiled and forgiven ourselves for that muddled attempt, but the discipling disaster turned into the beginning of my study through God's Word to discover what biblical mentoring should encompass. This preparation time— the year before Marni's letter arrived—gave me the opportunity to practice and refine what God was teaching me.

In this chapter and the next two we will examine the Titus directive. Entire books have been written on many of the subject areas within these three chapters, but I'll focus on useful tools and discussion ideas for both the discipler and the disciple. These thoughts on the Titus passage might serve as several weeks worth of study.

Let's take another look at the verses we'll be discussing:

> Then they can train the younger women to love their husbands and children, to be self-controlled and pure, to be busy at home, to be kind, and to be subject to their husbands, so that no one will malign the word of God (Titus 2:4, 5).

Train the Younger Woman

Hans Rookmaaker, Dutch art professor and founder of a Dutch L'Abri community, differentiates between students (taught ones) and disciples (trained ones). He believes that a student learns everything a teacher teaches her. But a disciple goes beyond that, taking the teacher's ideas and building on them.

The dictionary helps us to sense that training goes beyond teaching. *Train* means "to shape or develop the character of, by discipline or precept," "to grow (a plant) in a manner designed to produce a desired form or effect, usually by bending, tying, and pruning; especially to cause to grow symmetrically by such means."

Because I'm hopelessly addicted to growing all kinds of plants on our half acre, my imagination picked up on those gardening terms which depict a specific type of training. I could see that the encouraging of a mentor is like the careful nurturing of a gardener who provides good soil, water, and attention to his plants. The equipping of a woman equals the bending down and tying and pruning necessary for good growth. The desired reproducing of disciples from generation to generation reminds me of my efforts to propagate new "starts."

Train also reminds us of the outfitting of a ship for a long voyage or an army for battle (Ephesians 4:11-12). Discipling is equipping others for their journey and battles in life.

To Be Self-Controlled and Pure

Peter Marshall was a well-loved pastor and United States Senate Chaplain before his death in 1949. In one memorable sermon, "Keepers of the Springs," he challenged Christian women to reconsider a seemingly outdated morality. Pastor Marshall spoke out honestly, even bluntly:

> Our country needs today women who will lead us back to old-fashioned morality . . . to old-fashioned decency . . . to old-fashioned purity and sweetness . . . for the sake of the next generation, if for no other reason.[1]

Then Peter Marshall added his conviction that our world has enough women who are beautiful, smart, sophisticated, successful in careers, talented, and divorced—but how seldom we hear of a godly woman.

Purity and self-control do sound old-fashioned. Such people are an endangered species in our high-tech society. And the media unrelentingly chips away at our tolerance levels, reinforcing this sad situation.

But young women need to learn about self-control and purity, to be trained in the wisdom that leads to Christian values and conduct. Some come from homes where this was not the norm, and television soap operas have only emphasized promiscuity as the standard lifestyle choice. We need to talk openly about the "soaps" and their damage to a woman's attitudes and inner values. Masquerading as innocent time-killers, they actually work against the righteous living God desires for us. His standards for purity must be taken seriously.

But I also need to speak clearly and specifically about areas which yesterday's Christian woman didn't think much about—virginity before marriage (and fidelity during); drugs, alcohol, and other abuses of our bodies; divorce; abortion and many "new technology" options presented to infertile and pregnant women.

First Thessalonians 4:7 reminds believers that "God did not call us to be impure, but to live a holy life." In some translations of this passage, "a holy life" reads "in sanctification." Sanctification implies purity. I am to know myself well enough to avoid situations, people, and things that make me vulnerable to sin. Titus 2 women possess the kind of moral and spiritual integrity which overcomes moments of temptation. The whims and expectations of others won't fence us in if our words, our appetites and bodies, our thoughts and attitudes are well controlled.

I try to remember that self-control in and of itself doesn't remake me into a woman of excellence. It places me, however, where God can do His good work in me—where He can lovingly weave into my life old-fashioned words like *reverent, modest, discreet,* and *appropriate.* This sense of propriety will set boundary lines to all I say and do.

To Be Kind

A Japanese proverb suggests, "One kind word can warm three winter months." Our actions should be as kind as our words. As I think back to our earlier conclusions about doing good, I spot a strong correlation between kindness and goodness.

Kindness makes good on fine intentions. Let your spiritual daughter see you planning a picnic to share with a nursing home shut-in, or hear you offering to keep your neighbor's mischievous preschoolers while she gets a needed haircut and stocks up on groceries with a new-found sanity.

Kindness often shows genuine interest in the hobbies or avocation of another person. I'm sure that God also expects kindness to show up as frequently in the way we interact with our children as it does with our friends at church.

Kindness is also displayed in good manners. First Corinthians 13:5 states this succinctly by reminding us that "Love has good manners" (Phillips). Courtesy shows and tells others of our genuine concern for them. Let me suggest a few areas where I think we need to show more courtesy.

- Show concern for others (especially the unsaved and newcomers) by *not* saving seats, tables, beds— at concerts, banquets, camp facilities, workshops, etc.

- Write thank-you notes for kindnesses which have brightened your days. Our words say "I'm thinking of you and I care."

- After the speaker starts to speak, after the musician starts to sing, or after the Women's Fellowship president starts conducting business, bring all conversation to a halt.

- Show sensitivity and self-control by not swiveling our heads to see who is behind us or who might be coming in late.

The heart of all rudeness lies in selfishness, in not thinking of the other person. A list of discourtesies might include forgetting to line up a substitute Sunday school teacher; leaving the television on when someone stops by; interrupting when someone else is talking; habitually arriving late (this says my schedule must be more important than yours); edging ahead of someone in the line at the supermarket or the slow traffic line on the highway.

In Philippians 2:3-4 Paul gives an excellent definition of good manners and kindness:

Do nothing out of selfish ambition or vain conceit,
but in humility consider others better than yourselves.

81

What Is God Teaching Me in Titus 2?

> Each of you should look not only to your own interests, but also to the interests of others.

By the example of our lives and by our encouragement, we can show the younger woman what it means to be a godly woman. Because we have experienced God's grace and moment by moment support through the years of our own discouragements and crises, we have the privilege of passing on some of the lessons we've learned. Today's younger women face difficult, granite-hard situations. They need the special kind of encouragement and assurance promised in Hebrews 13:8, "Jesus Christ is the same yesterday and today and forever."

MORE WORTHY WOMAN IDEAS

1. Read Titus 2:3-5 (yes, again!) and decide why Paul included qualities such as self-control and discretion. Which individuals in the Bible seem to especially display these valuable qualities? What guidelines can you draw for yourself? What action can you take now?

2. Trace God's grace in your life by making a diagram or graph of your spiritual journey. Use dates and notations to define the particulars: What do you usually find associated with your "lows"? What went before or accompanied the high points of your walk with God?

3. Make a personal study of the Book of Proverbs, noting each reference to what we say and the way we say it. Then read James 1:26, 3:2-12, and 5:12. Which of the various "tongue troubles" mentioned in James and Proverbs hassle you most? Select one to work on for a month and make yourself accountable to someone else for this goal.

1. Catherine Marshall, *Mr. Jones, Meet the Master* (New York: Fleming H. Revell Co., 1951), p. 147.

7

BUT I KNOW HOW
TO LOVE MY HUSBAND—
DON'T I?

———————————————————————

F orty years ago my mother-in-law handed me some folksy
lines of advice. I accepted the truths and appreciated the
humor. But I also remember taking those concepts very
seriously—and feeling the guilt accumulate when I messed up
on one, then another. Here's the list she gave me:

Ten Commandments for Wives

I. Honor thy own womanhood, that thy days may be long
in the house which thy husband provideth for thee.

II. Expect not thy husband to give thee as many luxuries as thy father hath given thee after many years of hard labor and economies.

III. Forget not the virtue of good humor, for verily all that a man hath will he give for a woman's smile.

IV. Thou shalt not nag.

V. Thou shalt coddle thy husband, for verily every man loveth to be fussed over.

VI. Remember that the frank approval of thy husband is worth more to thee than the sidelong glances of many strangers.

VII. Forget not the grace of cleanliness and good dressing.

VIII. Permit no one to assure thee that thou art having a hard time of it; neither thy mother, nor thy sister, nor thy maiden aunt, nor any of thy kinfolk. Thou shalt not let another disparage thy husband.

IX. Keep thy home with all diligence, for out of it cometh the joys of thine old age.

X. Commit thy ways unto the Lord thy God, and thy children shall rise up and call thee blessed.

Rather than cold black words on throwaway paper, I needed a warm and experienced mentor to nurture that insecure wife of the late 1940s. But I realize the wisdom in those commandments and I've even developed a few more points of my own as I'm learning what loving my husband means.

TO LOVE THEIR HUSBANDS

Do you remember Marni's surprise when she learned that God's best for her life meant learning to love her husband? Most younger wives share Marni's incredulity. After all, they've committed themselves completely to that wonderful hunk of masculinity. Who needs someone to tell them about love?

Love can't be explained or learned through "Learning to Love 105" in the Accelerated Education Series. Our lives are more importantly affected by seeing love overflow from irresistible lifestyles.

Many young women remember only negative examples of married love in their own homes. Magazines and television shout that love comes when we use the right breath mints or buy our loved one the right gift. Singers sing and songwriters write unceasingly about love. Or about their concept of love.

Women have an urgent need to learn how to love according to God's pattern. Rather than a feeling, love is always a choice; an act of our will in which special feelings *follow*.

Understanding God's love needs to precede learning to love our husbands. As our sovereign Role Model, the Lord demonstrated the direction—the active giving and accepting and caring— our love should take: "God so loved the world that He gave His one and only Son."

This brand of love neither keeps books nor requires repayment with interest next month; it ignores measuring cups and computers and calendars and digital watches. This love will never be wasted—even the tiniest shredded remnant lives on long after we do.

Loving others with God's kind of love means taking on the characteristics we observe in Jesus' life, in the unselfish love He illustrated in the parable of the Good Samaritan (Luke 10:30- 37). Instead of stuffing gospel tracts into the folds of the injured man's robes, the good Samaritan tended his wounds before taking him to the inn for recovery. And this Samaritan paid in advance for the care of the stranger, asking to be billed for any balance due. This is not the kind of love we see much of these days.

Many other New Testament verses speak of Jesus' loving lifestyle. Jesus saw individuals as God intended them to be and treated them accordingly.

SEVEN IDEAS FOR LOVING MY HUSBAND GOD'S WAY

I consider the encouraging and teaching of younger women to love their husbands a key concept in mentoring. The growing edge for so many women, of all ages and situations in life, begins here. And the real test of a Spirit-filled life (Ephesians 5:18) comes in the marriage and family relationship (Ephesians 5:22 on).

Be forewarned: Younger women will look at the friendship you display with your own husband as the example and inspiration for being friends with their husbands.

Perhaps the ideas I've periodically written down—to move my own thoughts into gear as I've worked with young wives—will help you. But remember that this is only a starter set!

Loving my husband God's way . . .

1. *Depends on allowing my husband to have distinct, different, even debatable personality traits.*

Janelle married a man who attacks life with incredible optimism and gusto. His personality is a provocative contrast to her own quiet and thoughtful nature.

Margie's husband, Rich, chose to play devil's advocate at church business meetings and in discussions on the Christian Education Committee. No one doubted Rich's spirituality, but his outspoken manner (reflecting his unique temperament) often embarrassed soft-spoken, peace-loving Margie.

For both of these women, the adjusting and accepting, then the affirming of their husbands developed slowly and with difficulty.

Even when our husbands' interests, parents, temperament, hobbies, friends, and habits irritate, Janelle and Margie and I remind ourselves that these differences count toward making our husbands the special individuals we fell in love with.

2. *Depends on taking time just for my husband, making him feel important in my life, and making his "terrible, no-good day" better.*

Such as:

- Phoning him at work (unless this is definitely off limits) just to tell him I love him, and why. No problem-sharing allowed.
- Saying "You look especially nice today." Women aren't the only ones who thrive on admiration and applause.
- Writing some poetry (even if you're not a poet) about a recent weekend together or crisis or whatever brought us closer.
- Skimping a bit on the household and clothing purchases for several months in order to surprise him with that new fishing stuff he dubbed too expensive. Sacrifice walks hand in hand with love in marriage; sacrifice makes love grow up.

3. *Depends on not thrusting my expectations on him.*

Young wives tend to pile up unrealistic expectations for everything and everyone. Satan makes good use of the resulting discouragement. Chuck Swindoll once remarked, "When you pull out the thorn of expectation, you'll also be rid of disappointment."[1]

Sometimes a young married woman sighs that her husband isn't meeting her needs or that he "isn't the spiritual leader he should be in our home." These women need to turn their expectations over to God instead of wishing their husbands were different. You and I must make responsible, *individual* choices before God.

To really love someone is to trust in him continually. As soon as we start judging, or heaping expectations on our husbands, we also start cutting him down. Slowly but surely he dwindles in our confidence and in his own. Gradually our love also dwindles, and he finds it impossible to change in any direction but down.

And I must not let my natural pride in my husband make me overly sensitive to his public image; this easily ripens into a selfish pride. Too often I want him to look good (at church, with colleagues and friends) so I will look good.

Love *dependent* on my husband's words or actions or charisma is no love at all.

4. Depends on being obedient to my husband in more than theory.

Using the whole Bible perspective, rather than scattered verses, I need to study what God intends for wives. What does it mean to obey my husband?

God never told us, "Wives obey your husbands, except when he . . ." So God's precept remains valid even when I believe the man I married is mistaken. While maintaining my own integrity, obeying my husband implies support and enthusiasm.

Personal integrity will not allow any violation of either God's commands or my own conscience. A few women struggle daily—either with something their husband asks them to do or with going with him to places which degrade their Christian principles. I try to give these women needed and ongoing support, as well as help to sort out genuine violations of conscience from a non-submissive spirit.

1 Peter 3:1-4 speaks of our behavior as worthy women:

> Wives, in the same way be submissive to your husbands so that, if any of them do not believe the word, they may be won over without talk by the behavior of their wives, when they see the purity and reverence of your lives. Your beauty should not come from outward adornment, such as braided hair and the wearing of gold jewelry and fine clothes. Instead it should be that of your inner self, the unfading beauty of a gentle and quiet spirit, which is of great worth in God's sight.

Have you ever stopped to ask yourself what is meant by "in the same way"? I recently paused over those words for the first time and found I needed to go back and read chapter 2 again. Then the pieces began to fit together better. Verse 21 and following remind us that we are to love "in the same way" as Christ loved. He is our example.

Give these verses a run-through yourself, and ask the Holy Spirit to show you new truth as you study.

And remember daily the tremendous role that male ego plays in marriage. God continues to teach me that a man must mostly learn things for himself. In view of the serious responsibilities lined out for husbands in Ephesians 5:25-33, do I allow my beloved the privilege of learning from his own mistakes? I must also remember the contradiction of obedience with clenched teeth.

5. *Depends on encouraging his male friendships.*

Today men are generally bereft of these relationships; they don't cultivate or nurture friendships in the way most women do.

Although I'm unsure of all the reasons for this lack, part of the problem seems tied to the demands of the corporation and the job. By the time the average American husband gets home, little time remains for his family and for completing the work he brought home in his briefcase, let alone for building friendships.

Women tell me they often tire of trying to substitute for those male friends, year in and year-out. But rather than just shaking our heads over the situation, you and I will encourage his friendships with other men by refraining from playing the martyr's role when he *does* plan a weekend fishing trip or regular bowling dates with the guy next door.

Since the wife is often the one who plans social times, you can choose couples with a husband who shares common interests with yours or whom your husband enjoys.

6. *Depends on realizing that God designed me to assist my husband in attaining his goals.*

Clutching at my husband's time or nagging about it never helps. It may only delay his homecoming because of the spoken or unspoken tirade he dreads. Few husbands deliberately neglect their wives, although many allow legitimate obligations to devour more time than is necessary.

I've been a super-slow learner in this department.

7. Depends on listening to him.

Meeting this basic need to be heard and understood by at least one other person allows maturity and God's fullness of joy to unfold in my husband's life.

This requires turning off my thoughts to concentrate totally on what my husband is saying and feeling so I can correctly hear the meaning behind the words. This may mean asking questions which clarify both meaning and feelings. And I need to remember that silence isn't always golden—sometimes it's a downright cowardly cop-out because at that moment an answer is important to him.

Expressing our struggles to someone we love often clears the fuzzies from our minds and becomes therapeutic. But being a good listener takes self-discipline. No shortcuts are allowed. Too quickly the glib advice, the implied judgment, or the urge to talk about self rushes to unloose our tongues.

Listening must be with my eyes and minds, as well as with my ears. This kind of listening will lead me to apologize freely, taking any blame and giving in at times. Caring communication never manipulates or plays games; it plays no subtle guilt trips on my man.

Husbands appreciate our input and feedback as long as our motives are honest. I want to be his friend and lover, not his Holy Spirit.

> If we are to progress in the spiritual walk ... we must come to the place in our lives where we lay down the everlasting burden of needing to manage others. ... When we genuinely believe that inner transformation is God's work and not ours, we can put to rest our passion to set others straight.[2]

MORE WORTHY WOMAN IDEAS

1. Study 1 Peter 2:9-3:8 and Ephesians 5:21-6:9 before drawing up your personal/biblical rationale for submission to your husband. What additional Scripture can you find on the subject?

2. What specific improvements in communication (especially listening) would build up your personal relationships—with boss and co-workers? Children? Friends? Husband? Parents? Church leaders? Neighbors? Write down at least one for each applicable relationship.

3. Read *Lovelife* by Ed Wheat, M.D. (Grand Rapids, Mich.:Zondervan Publishing House, 1980).

1. Charles E. Swindoll, from a message at Mount Hermon Bible Conference, Mount Hermon, CA, July 1981.
2. Richard J. Foster, *Celebration of Discipline* (New York: Harper and Row, 1978), p. 8.

8

DOES GOD REALLY WANT ME TO STAY AT HOME?

I 've not worked outside my home since I married Bob. Even the mixed discipline and delight of freelance writing these past seven years allows me to work at home 95 percent of the time. God seems to have given me a tempera- ment well suited to the climate of home and family; that's what He has in mind for me.

For you it may be another story.

When Libby asked me some years ago if I had ever regret- ted my stay-at-home status, I didn't have an answer. I honestly hadn't thought much about it, one way or another. Now I realize that God used other people to provide the challenge I might have missed and hungered for if I had limited myself to changing diapers and beds or to checking the accuracy of recited multiplication tables and Scripture verses.

My years of actively participating in my church's missions and Christian education programs (Sunday school, VBS, Pioneer Girls club, etc.) probably sound much like your own. But serving on our denomination's state Christian Education Commission for several years provided a further outlet for my creativity. Among other things, I planned and made arrangements for mini-Sunday school conferences in remote corners of Oregon.

Most women do need challenging and worthwhile work, whether in or out of the home. Back in 1850 Florence Nightingale lamented, "I offered the church my heart, my mind, and all my life, but it sent me to do crochet work in my grandmother's parlor."

You and I have felt that kind of frustration sometimes, haven't we? But rather than stumbling over a problem that belongs more rightfully to others, we should remain available, offering ourselves in the way Florence Nightingale did.

Our wise Heavenly Father who gave us those seemingly clear and simple directives in Titus 2 knows us and our circumstances even better than we do. So let's allow Him the time and space and opportunity to suggest creative solutions to our dilemmas.

IS IT LESS SPIRITUAL TO WORK OUTSIDE THE HOME?

When Margie broached the idea of returning to the teaching position she left a year after her marriage to Rich, he replied, "If I had wanted some other woman to raise my kids, I think I would have married her."

The question of keeping busy in a career or at home perplexes many Christian women. And each home situation is different—as different as each woman and each man married to that woman.

But when Titus 2:5 speaks of our being workers or keepers at home, I sense that diligent attention must be given the place I call home. This includes discovering and keeping the right balance between job, church, family and friends, home, neighbors and loving attention to husband and kids.

Recent statistics highlight a rapidly increasing number of mothers who work beyond the home. Fifty-three percent of moms with young children now participate in the labor force. Their generation has grown up expecting to have a career or job. Economics currently dictates that many women must work—to provide the second income which seems necessary to continue the high mortgage payments and keep the children in music lessons and orthodontic treatment.

Passages like Deuteronomy 4:9 and Titus 2:5 suggest that God intended for women to be at home with their children. But what about the biblical exceptions like Priscilla, Deborah, Lydia, and the Proverbs 31 woman? The Bible doesn't specifically say all these women had children, but it would have been the exception in that culture not to have children.

When we observe the many contemporary and worthy women working away from home at least part of the time, what rationale can we claim in teaching this section of Titus? As a role model and disciplemaker who learns along with her younger friends, my own perspective on this subject has recently been helped by Patricia Rushford's words:

> We have an appeal from God to build our home and maintain order there (Titus 2:5). We also have an appeal from God in other parts of Scripture to use our unique gifts and talents, to feed the hungry and clothe the naked, to uplift, encourage, and support others. And finally, we have the ultimate task of making disciples of all nations.
>
> So, when we explore the Scriptures as a whole, women are not simply lumped together in one batch of clay. God did not mass produce us as vessels with one purpose and engrave us with the name "Homemaker". . . .

We don't stay home because the Bible says we should, and we don't work out of the home because the Bible says we should. The Bible shows women in various situations. Consequently, the answer as to whether or not you should be working is strictly between you and your family and God.[1]

Remembering that God created each of us, uniquely and beautifully, I want to suggest these three considerations:

1. Some Christian women possess great potential for leadership and serving outside the home. This out-of-the-ordinary gift should not be allowed to stagnate or wither from disuse.

2. Often God equips and enables these women to effectively hold an outside job while being equally effective at home. Think of this woman's potentially great influence in both worlds.

3. Women with unusual abilities and energies do not violate God's injunctions to be a submissive wife and busy at home unless they fail to carry out their first-given assignments, unless they get their priorities disarranged. Notice that Paul didn't tell women to "stay at home" (perhaps to watch the television or to gossip on the telephone), but advised us to keep busy at home.

MAKING THE CHOICE

When a young woman weighs the pros and cons of a job or a career, I often suggest that she ask herself:

- Is there some way I can work at home or out of my home? This eliminates the need to pay for a babysitter and cuts down on the cost of wardrobe and transportation expenses.

- Can I tighten my budget? This works better than earning more income because it means less taxes to pay.

- Why do I want to work outside my home? How

will this match my goals in six months? In ten to fifteen years?

- Am I qualified for the job I have in mind? Will I have to bring my job home at times?
- In what way will this change glorify God?
- What arrangements am I sure I can make for my children's care, any training needed, my husband's welfare, etc?
- Does my husband totally agree that this will be an okay thing for me to do?

These questions might also be asked when contemplating a new ministry at church or a different volunteer work in the community.

TO LOVE THEIR CHILDREN

Part of keeping busy at home includes mothering. Despite the plethora of parenting books, most of us feel inadequate for the task. God, speaking through Paul, commands us to teach younger women how to love their children.

How do you and I teach this?

I'm including a lesson plan here, so you can see how I prepared for and covered the Titus section about learning to love our children. You will have additional material of your own to include later.

Lesson Plan for October 21

Focus:
Titus 2:3-5 Learning to love your children

Praise and Worship: Psalm 78:1-7
Read aloud and emphasize God's command to teach and rehearse his sovereignty and mighty deeds. Emphasize the importance of obedience from both adults and kids.

Encouragement and Prayer:
Include new needs and praise. My magazine article is

99

finished! Ask Laura to pray for and later check back on my afternoon with my neighbor.

Accountability and Goals:

Check on Laura's quiet times this past week and her goals for affirming her husband. Does Tim communicate more?

Study:

Learning to love children by learning their needs

1. Build a strong sense of family with traditions and ritual:

   a. Homemade valentine and birthday cards b. Make Dutch Babies (or another favorite) every Saturday morning c. Have a jigsaw puzzle spree between Christmas and New Year's day d. Continually laugh together over family stories and love each relative individually.

   Youngest and oldest are always VIPs. Read Psalm 78:1-7 again and Deuteronomy 11:18-21.

2. Family models

   Parents are primary models for kids, but parents and families also need models. Ask: What do you want your family to be like? How do you feel about your family? Which families serve as models for your family? Which mom models for you?

   I've chosen personal role models who are strong in areas where I feel weak.

3. Shared laughter and fun

   Value of laughing *with* kids; value of family jokes and catch words which occur spontaneously when the family is together. Give examples from our family. Tell Laura about granddaughter watching hot dogs cook—"They're getting sweaty, Grandma."

4. Encouragement and confidence building, listening.

   Kids thrive on praise, appreciation, and applause (single out one as "special person" for a day or hour). Encouragement inspires self-confidence. One of my role models told me long ago, "If at all possible, give your kids yes answers to build confidence and to let them know you trust them."

Each child must be loved as she is; our disappointment is easily sensed. *Cherish* is an excellent word and attitude (look up meaning together).

When mom drops to knees and gives total attention, it shows she isn't too important or grown up to get down on child's level; great way to communicate "I love you."

Look for listening opportunities at bedtime, on shopping excursion with one child at a time, taking walks to find first pussy willows of spring, etc.

5. A mom who has her priorities straight focuses on them instead of the trivial.

Let children know God comes first (do they see your joyful friendship with Him?) . . . their dad comes next (do they know you love him unconditionally?) . . . children come next (not SS department you lead, or medical secretary job you go to part-time, or immaculate house?)

Kids also need a mom who understands the importance of letting go gradually and early enough. When I compared the long lists of rules and commandments in the Old Testament with the simple and beautiful precept of love in the New Testament, I saw similarity to our parental responsibilities. Rules must be there for guidance and foundation, but should be supplanted gradually or superseded by the primary law of love.

Read together Psalm 90:12; remind Laura she has less than forever to nurture and train her children, to love their dad, and to influence others. Share my "hindsight experience."

Assignment:
Read about Jochebed (Moses' mother), Sarah, Hannah, Eunice and Mary (Jesus' mother). What traits did they have in common?

Make up a list for each child of things you want to do with them one-on-one over the next three months. Note specific dates by at least one idea for each child.

How To Keep "Busy At Home"

Disciplemakers may discover that some young women need definite instructions about the art of keeping a home clean and organized for their families, about cooking and preserving seasonal food for the winter seasons of their year, about budgeting and buying wisely. The basics of good diet and nutrition, and much more, enter this domestic scenario.

I've never come right out and asked, "Are you a good housekeeper?" But I'm afforded a small opening for questions and statements when my discipling partner and I talk about goals. I urge her to estimate her own housekeeping skills, then I wonder aloud if she wants to set some definite goals for changes.

Later I might say: "I would really enjoy sharing your home setting next week. Could we meet at your house for lunch? I'll bring a salad big enough for both of us."

Sometimes I've already been in her home and usually I've had opportunities to observe her relationship with her husband and her children. But I also remember "it is only with the heart that one can see rightly; what is essential is invisible to the eye."[2]

With one young woman I felt housekeeping might be a sensitive area, but she voiced a need for help. So I asked if my friend Betsy could be her resource person. Step by patient step, Betsy shared her twenty-three years of "at home" experience, right down to the shortcuts.

This worked so well that I want to emphasize the concept of utilizing other women as resource people. I want the young women I disciple to observe and absorb the values of other Christian role models, of other godly women with strengths and areas of expertise I don't have. For example, I'm at the bottom of the heap when it comes to sewing and craft skills, so I've drawn one of my nimble-fingered friends into assisting when the need arises. And I turn to my friend Lorraine, with her library know-how, for help in selecting appropriate books.

I've met women who consider the idea of creating and keeping a happy, comfortable home environment too mundane a focus in training younger women. But have you ever noticed that a dirty, disorderly home plays havoc with a woman's feelings of self-respect? Check it out.

I believe a strong correlation exists between the inner woman and her outer self—the way she dresses and keeps her house and speaks to her children. A disciplined and obedient lifestyle positively affects her thoughts and attitudes; sloppy grooming and housekeeping usually trigger sloppy ways of thinking and living.

HOMEMAKERS AREN'T BORN THAT WAY

An increased need for attention to homemaking skills exists in this generation: Many women aren't learning about cooking and cleaning from their natural mothers.

Most of those mothers worked full-time outside their home and had little time for housework and cooking. Mostly they worked at it after the children were in bed for the night. Food purchasing usually boiled down to a quick pit stop for groceries on the way home from the job. Those moms had less time to patiently show their daughters the how-to of homemaking and to work alongside those apprentice homemakers. They weren't available after school to applaud or encourage on the spot the completion of chores from the "to do" list on the refrigerator.

Instead of learning from their mothers, many adolescent daughters were busy rebelling. They avoided the classroom of the cleaning supply cupboard because peer group affirmation seemed all-important.

Tina needed to learn the basics of housekeeping—planning tentative menus and making good grocery lists and using the food ads (plus coupons) to cut costs. She needed someone to show her how to effectively and regularly clean her bathroom, her refrigerator, and closets. Because Tina longed to somehow beautify her small home, my suggestions of buying inexpensive houseplants and displaying her great-grandmother's lovely quilt came as new and helpful ideas.

Our Lord wants us to understand the value of the homemaking tasks He gives us. Proverbs 24:3-4 emphasizes:

> By wisdom a house is built, and through understanding it is established; through knowledge its rooms are filled with rare and beautiful treasures.

Titus 2 women need to realize that keeping a clean and cheerful home is no more optional than working hard at keeping marriage fresh and strong. They need to glimpse the incredible fulfillment available to "keepers at home" and the greater outreach possible to neighborhood children and families.

Janelle affirmed the importance of these qualities when she wrote:

> I can see that it was my respect for you—as a total person, not isolating the spiritual—which gave your words and actions such import. Respect for your creativity, your mind, your relationship with your husband, the way you kept your house and garden, and little things (like noticing a book of my favorite author's poems in your living room), all made you so easy to imprint on my mind and heart.

One pleasant facet of the homemaking concept is God's emphasis on hospitality. Four years ago my husband and I lived briefly in Australia. Bob and I attended a church in a neighboring village, but one weekend we visited another church north of Melbourne. As visitors from America we frequently received Sunday dinner invitations from hospitable Aussie believers. Our meal with the Horners stands out, though, as true hospitality.

The Horners had moved back to Australia only a few days before our visit. But their goods hadn't arrived, and the family was temporarily living in a cold, unfurnished house which was slated for demolition.

Our hostess rummaged through two boxes of donated groceries and added borrowed utensils while we perched on upended boxes at a too-small kitchen table. The bread, cheese, and fruit she spread before us, accompanied by traditional cups of milky tea, made as fine a meal as I can recall in that country of kangaroos and gum trees.

Why? Because we laughed and shared our common joys and sorrows throughout the meal. Because the three children showed genuine pleasure in our visit. The hospitality was authentic—from the heart and for the Lord. It was the kind of hospitality I want younger women to understand and practice.

The speaking notes and handout sheet I'ved used in several hospitality workshops served as a good outline when Mary Jo and others wanted to talk about hospitality. (They appear at the end of the chapter.)

Colossians 3:12 says, ". . . you should practice tenderhearted mercy and kindness to others. Don't worry about making a good impression on them" (TLB). This gives me the freedom to relax and enjoy myself and my guests; all the Lord requires is my availability. So don't apologize for the house or overcooked peas or whatever, because that only draws attention to it.

Our homes belong to the Lord because we belong to Him. We can count on His helpful support and insight along the way as we start reaching out through hospitality. I've enjoyed seeing some women think of new ways to involve their children in plans for hospitality as well as in other matters that make being busy at home a rather pleasant prospect!

MORE WORTHY WOMAN IDEAS

1. Think through and write out your personalized reason for obeying God's words about keeping "busy at home." In what way will you put this into action? Talk with your husband about your choices, and plan to re-evaluate every three years or so. Read Philippians 1:9-10 and make it your prayer.

2. Use either the hospitality or homemaking guidelines in this chapter to make up a lesson plan for discipling.

3. Read 1 Corinthians 13:4-13 slowly, applying the love precepts to your children. What quality do you most need to work on as a mom for at least the next month?

1. Patricia H. Rushford, *What Kids Need Most In a Mom* (Old Tappan, NJ: Fleming H. Revell Co., 1986), p. 173.
2. Antoine De Saint-Exupery, *The Little Prince* (New York: Harcourt, Brace and World, Inc., 1943), p. 70.

Hospitality without Hassle

I. Purposeful hospitality adds to our pleasure.

A. Pray ahead about the "who and when."

B. Invite far enough ahead for comfort but not for forgetting. Include specifics like "wear casual clothes," "your kids are included" (or not). Ask guest to let you know if last-minute problem cancels their coming. Even among Christians no-shows aren't unusual.

C. Get date onto calendar immediately, along with any helpful details.

D. Invite to discover the delights of people-putting-together (similar interests, hometown, jobs, ages of children, church ministry, etc.)

E. Invite with a creative, age-leveling perspective. Get involved with all kinds of people and age levels— elderly, college students, missionaries, neighbors, singles, marrieds, co-workers and boss, newcomers.

II. Essentials for enjoying hospitality.

A. Advance preparation (known as AP from now on) is the key. Ideally, two-thirds of food preparation should be done ahead, kept in freezer or refrigerator.

(1) Prayer important part of AP; pray for guests, conversation, timing, etc. God can then work out his best hospitality and people-plans through you. Do ahead all that will allow you to give your heart and mind to people, not details of food and serving.

(2) Lists invaluable:

a. Food list—check recipes and inventory staples; amounts needed? Shop ahead.

b. Menu list—itemize everything, including serving dishes to use, seating, etc. Make last-minute check before guests are seated.

c. Do-ahead list—include most cleaning, all food preparation possible, and table set the night before (if you have a place for your family to eat!).

       d. Last-minute list—times listed for showering, casserole in oven, start fixing salad, candles lit, etc.

B. You make people feel comfortable (yourself too!) by:

     (1) Being a good listener, asking lots of questions.

     (2) Genuinely enjoying people of all ages and stages.

     (3) Experimenting with room and furniture arrangement; evaluating what works best for group dynamics and traffic.

     (4) Sometimes playing games, especially with a mixed age or interest group. Games must be simple-to-learn and nonthreatening.

     (5) Adding warmth with soft background music.

     (6) Always putting people ahead of food and cleaning.

III. Buffet is often the best way to handle more than ten to twelve people.

A. Make sketch and think through the traffic flow and seating and table arrangement. I still do this with a large or unfamiliar group.

B. Consider eye appeal—contrasting textures, colors, hot and cold. Use garnishes like parsley, fresh mint, citrus slices, even a freshly-picked leaf accent from outdoors.

C. Avoid using any food that will wilt or be less than its best if meal is delayed a bit.

D. Putting beverages at separate table often smooths the traffic congestion.

E. Choose unusual containers to serve foods in—this adds interest.

F. Line up a helper or two—good way to make a new person feel at ease.

G. Evaluate afterward, using file cards with how much food was actually used, dated menu with names of guests and any food taboos, etc.

IV. Miscellaneous thoughts:

A. If wary about plunging into hospitality, start small and easy; use recipes you know well and include one or two friends when inviting.

B. Keep your eyes open at other homes to see how they do it, to absorb ideas—but never compare.

C. Decide on your own hospitality priorities—what brings the most pleasure for you and your family? Hospitality also happens without food sometimes.

D. Simplify. For example, let guests help themselves by setting out airpot with hot water and fixings (tea and coffee assortment, perhaps cocoa and spiced apple drink packets). I find a big pitcher of ice-water gets used more than commercial soft drinks or fancy punch.

E. Substitute flair for money and time—try sheets for tablecloths; use lots of baskets, candles, pitchers; group several candles of varying sizes.

F. Centerpiece can be last minute—autumn leaves or ivy laid on table; fresh fruit or veggies in basket with leaves or greens; houseplant.

G. Let others bring part of meal—gulp down that bit of false pride so others can minister to you too. If the offer is made, accept it gratefully.

H. When unsure of compatibility of guests (or for other reasons), plan "built-in time limit" by using one of the ideas below, such as meal before planned church or sports event.

I. Hospitality is the best friendship-builder ever, so enjoy!

V. Creative hospitality may include:

A. Saturday or Sunday breakfast; Saturday brunch in yard.

B. A soup party—you furnish two soups or chowders, beverage; friends can bring cheeses, breads, and desserts.

C. An invitation to a picnic beside the television during the BIG game.

D. Progressive potluck at three or four homes, with all helping with food.

E. Dessert party, inviting just for dessert—chance to try that fancy one!

F. Two or three families put meal together from what they have on hand—"I've got leftover roast and cake. What can you bring?"

G. Simple brunch or coffee for bridal or baby shower or birthday.

H. A simple meal before home Bible study or missionary conference program.

I. A spur-of-the-moment picnic with family of one of your child's Sunday school friends.

J. A morning "coffee" for visiting missionary, old friend, or newcomer.

K. Get to know new people at church by inviting them over after Sunday evening church or before church business meeting or following choir's special event.

L. Themes can be fun for gatherings—Mexican Piñata Party, Election Night Special, Hawaiian Luau, Housewarming Shower, Chinese New Year.

VI. Menu ideas we have liked . . . and they meet AP requirements!

Breakfast or Brunch: orange-coconut sweet rolls, cheesy scrambled eggs, ham or sausages done in oven, fruit from freezer, coffee.

Family-style dinner: lasagna, fruit or jello salad, fresh vegetable, warmed french or garlic bread, berry cobbler, beverage.

or

barbecued oven chicken,
scalloped potatoes, fancy
green bean casserole (all
cook in oven at same
time), relish plate of raw
veggies, ice cream or
fresh fruit dessert.

"Just Girls" Lunch

chili-chicken and cheese
casserole, tossed green
salad, banana bread, ice
cream pie, beverage.

"Guys Too" Lunch

taco salad, chips and
cracker assortment,
cinnamon rolls, fresh
fruit plate, apple crisp,
beverage.

Sunday Night Snacks:

popcorn and fruit punch
and cheese nibbles.

fresh veggies, chips and
crackers, beverage.

small rolls (purchased)
filled with sandwich stuff,
plate of fresh fruit,
chips, beverage.

strawberry shortcake (or
just berries on ice
cream).

granola and/or natural
nuts and seeds, fruit salad.

your favorite coffeecake
(made earlier and
reheated), Russian tea
and coffee and cocoa,
or root beer floats

9

DOES DISCIPLEMAKING WORK WELL IN SMALL GROUPS?

S ometimes—especially when the marigolds bloom—I look back to what I think of as The Significant Year. Not because of any major move or changes in finances or circumstances, not even because of milestones in the lives of our children. The significance exists because 1980 registered profoundly on the barometer of my deep-down Christian growth. Through discipling three very special women, I discovered the value of personal vulnerability and accountability that year.

Does Disciplemaking Work Well in Small Groups?

Small group discipling can be an especially effective and encouraging way of nurturing women. Both older and younger women may feel less threatened in a love knot of three to six. The focus seems less concentrated on any one person and a greater amount of sharing usually materializes.

Oh, you wondered about the marigolds? They are descendants of the marigold seed Elise brought each of our group on May Day of 1980. Marigolds from generation to generation!

THE ADVANTAGES OF SMALL GROUPS

Mutual nurturing and accountability takes on an even deeper dimension among several like-minded women. An atmosphere of mutual confidentiality and trust becomes a strong, dynamic focus.

Praise and worship usually come more easily within a group. It certainly feels more comfortable to sing our praises in a quartet or sextet than a duet. The words of Scripture set to music in a hymn or chorus prompt sensitivity to the Lord's presence. Many hymnals contain readings which complement the hymns and tie in well with the different topics or Bible sections we are discussing.

Discussion flows easier. The Proverbs 27:17 truth, "As iron sharpens iron, so one [woman] sharpens another," glows appropriately here. I've often seen one woman's questions spark answers and stimulate questions in another's mind. This snowball effect broadens the responsibility for facilitating group discussion. If the discipler isn't greatly gifted with social or teaching skills, this shared leading comes as a blessing.

Within a smaller group it seems easier to not only learn to know God better, but also to learn to know other women better. Many younger women need to improve their expertise in relationships, both vertically and horizontally. Sharing probably comes more spontaneously and frequently within a group of three to five. In our group we shared so much—from Elise's marigold seed and poems and Bible treasures and recipes, to our deepest heart-needs. So many memories smile at each other!

114

A small group offers women the opportunity for familiarity with a few leadership training skills. Mentors will want to ask themselves, "What does each young woman need to know; what does she need to do?" Those with leadership ability should be given the opportunity to lead some of your meetings.

Praying happens more spontaneously with three or four others and it's easier to pray effectively. Someone else within the group often becomes a part of answered prayer. Women not only help in bearing one another's burdens (both in prayerful and practical ways), but also find help for bearing their own burden in a God-honoring way.

Forever friendships make up the end product of this small circle's caring and praying, forming almost family-like bonds.

C.S. Lewis evaluates true friendship within the Christian context—a standard which would surely enhance all our relationships—by suggesting:

> But for a Christian, there are, strictly speaking, no "chances." A secret Master of Ceremonies has been at work. Christ, who said to the disciples, "Ye have not chosen me, but I have chosen you," can say truly to every group of Christian friends, "You have not chosen one another but I have chosen you for one another." The friendship is not a reward for our discrimination and good taste in finding one another out. . . . At *this* feast, it is He who has spread the board and it is He who has chosen the guests. It is He, we may dare to hope, who sometimes does (and always should) preside. Let us not reckon without our Host.[1]

At the time our discipling group of four met, I'm not sure anyone thought about group dynamics or the reasons our small gathering worked so well. We just thanked God for the growing and sparkling friendships and for the worthy-woman precepts we were learning.

How Do I Structure A Group?

Before our group was formed, two of the women had discussed wanting to do something like this. They came to me with the idea. I believe this might be the best way because the initiative shown by the younger women indicates genuine interest and commitment.

But I can't rule out an older woman feeling strongly about starting a small group and then asking those women the Holy Spirit brings to mind. Be sure the women seem compatible and that a good balance will exist within the small group. If several individuals have strong personalities, one-on-one mentoring or another group may be better for them. Again, ask God for wisdom.

We followed the same basic but loose elements I mentioned in Chapter 4: praise and worship; encouragement and prayer; accountability and goals; study and discussion. I learned that a spiritual agenda wasn't always what was most needed. Sometimes the Holy Spirit urged me to forget my plans and just listen.

Our high level of involvement with one another called for meeting together from 9:30 A.M. until noon each Thursday. At times, the young women—and one winsome new baby—stayed on for a planned potluck lunch. Sharing recipes and meals brought us even closer together.

The basics of disciplemaking with more than one woman remain much the same as those we've discussed for one-on-one mentoring. I always try to prepare these discipling partners for making responsible choices in a sometimes irresponsible world. Many of the pressing choices will relate to age and will tie in with the current season of that woman's life.

A Closer Look at a Small Group

Yesterday I leafed through the pages of my notes from that years-ago group. Today it occurs to me that some of you would like to glimpse what we did together. Not because the needs or interests or temperaments of your small group would even halfway match, but because looking over my shoulder may give you more of a feel for this lovely ministry and relationship.

In the beginning the four of us focused on the reason for this kind of nurturing group, on Jesus and His disciples, and other foundational material you've already read in earlier chapters. I also asked for these commitments:

- Let nothing short of a crisis keep you from our weekly sessions (this group managed a 100% attendance record.)
- Bring Bible, notebook, and any homework assigned.
- Be praying for and in touch with the others during the week.

The random notes which follow come from other drawing-together times. (Confidentiality disallows disclosure of the shared praises, prayer requests, goals, and conversation of our group—the heart and center of my notes!)

April 3rd session. Talked about priorities—where each of us positions husband, job, church, children, Christ, housework, small personal priorities. The order of some (but not all) may change with passing years. Which?

Read in Romans 7:15, 24 about Paul's frustration. Talked about goals needing to be measurable and attainable. Read Proverbs 16:9. What do Jeremiah 29:11 and Psalm 138:8 say to us about goal-setting and striving?

Handed out charts to fill in this week and bring back next time—went over a sample to see how it works.

April 10th session. Since our group goal is loving one another and those close to us we began with praise and shared several "love verses" from the Bible. Handed out references to look up and read, then closed with 1 Corinthians 13 in Phillips' paraphrase. Praise included real progress in seeing ourselves as we really are. Prayer time.

Using our individual goals as a basis each one shared and freely discussed her goals. All are using notebooks, taking notes often, and feel excited about what is happening in group.

May 8th session. Began with Elise's "praise notes" and Karen's "inflation-fighting hints" which tied in with topic of money and financial discernment. Looked up and discussed 1 Peter 4:7-11 (noticed that giving is just part of the whole), and 2 Corinthians 8:1-15 in Phillips'paraphrase. Read poem about stewardship and discussed the parable of the talents in Matthew 25:14-29. None of us can claim exception from accountability!

Gave out sheet with biblical principles for investing money. Suggested that women share with husbands (even if it didn't seem needful currently), remembering parable and balancing it with "lay not up treasures . . ." passage. Read quote on thrift.

My notes help me evaluate what to do the next week and serve as a reminder of prayer requests.

CHARACTERISTICS OF A HEALTHY SUPPORT GROUP

If a spiritual mentor doesn't ask for commitment and change, the small discipling group becomes almost beside the point. That's one reason I've emphasized the value of goals and accountability: living a life wide open to change.

How does the older woman ask for change and commitment? I like the phrase "prescription ministry," used by Jay Carty (he conducts workshops on evangelism, renewal, and discipleship throughout the western states).

Jay spoke about a man named Sam who discipled him with a carefully planned and prepared series of spiritual exercises which were never optional. Jay said: "It was part of Sam's plan. He cared about me—so much, in fact, that he thought through the recipe necessary to take me from baby food to steak. Sam wrote my prescription."

Although I've already stressed fitting the mentoring to the individual, the concept of writing each woman's prescription gives a face to what I'm talking about. We older women can determine points of needed growth in our younger friends and can then write their prescription through the plans and challenges we suggest for them and support them in.

In the assignments for dealing with Marni's anger and improving Mary Jo's self-image, you have seen some examples of prescription-writing. Another one read like this:

> *Rx for Laura:* Check out from a church library at least two books on improving communication skills. Then write into your notebook the author's points which you feel will especially help you. Each week select a different one to practice and let me know what happens.

Well thought-out prescriptions can lead to healthy growth.

The Christmas after my first group discipling experience, I appreciated seeing special "growth marks" in those young women. Caryn decided to carry on a holiday tradition of her husband's family—making Christmas bread-wreaths and delivering them to friends and family with her husband. Elise lovingly cared for an older neighbor lady, even though it curtailed some of her own holiday plans. And Karen wrote this poem, gifting each of her discipling friends with a copy:

> friends
>> in Christ,
>> in my heart
>> I see you
>> like a hill-full of flowers
>> in spring—
>>> yellow,
>>>> lavender,
>>>>> white—
>> all shades of colors,
>>> reaching tall
>> and spreading close to the ground;
>>> budding,
>>> blooming,
>>>> brightly
>> in the glorious light
>>> of the Son.[2]

As I've thought about Karen's lovely word-picture of the kind of friendship which grows and blooms between believers, I consider it a fitting round of applause—and a strong fringe benefit—for the small group kind of nurturing.

MORE WORTHY WOMAN IDEAS

1. Read chapters 1-3 of 1 Thessalonians, especially noting and listing Paul's strategy for keeping newly discipled people strong in the faith. For instance, in 1:2-3 Paul expresses the appreciation new and growing Christians need to hear. Go on from there and find specific ways he continues his role modeling and mentoring.

2. Do you sense God's strong desire that you lead a small group? Consider which two or three younger women God might want you to gather into a group. After praying about those names, go to one and suggest the idea. If the response is positive, suggest that this woman talk with the others, unless you prefer to go to them yourself.

3. Paul's words in Colossians 3:12-16 seem ideally suited as guidelines for a small discipling group. Write out a para-

phrase in your own words, after reading them in several translations of the Bible.

1. C.S. Lewis, *The Four Loves* (New York: Harcourt Brace Jovanovich, Inc., 1960), pp. 126, 127.
2. Karen McCord, © 1980.

10

HOW DO I BALANCE COUNSELING WITH DISCIPLING?

———————————————————————

Stephanie turned and quietly asked me (in the same voice she had used earlier to ask the time), "Next week could we talk about marriage? Mine just isn't working." Then she quickly moved to her car and drove away.

This young woman's extreme shyness had already posed a challenge during our previous four afternoons of meeting together. But that day I felt she was finally more comfortable with hearing her own voice as we studied "friendship." I hadn't the slightest idea that inside, Stephanie churned and wrestled

123

with problems which her calm exterior didn't even hint at.

I realized that for a few weeks I would become a counselor as we delved into the problems in her marriage. Although I felt inadequate to help her, I knew that the Holy Spirit is adequate. Always.

WHY DO I BELIEVE I CAN HELP THIS PERSON?

When trying to decide whether I can help a woman such as Stephanie with her problem, I often try to determine if her situation matches one of the following guidelines. If so, I feel encouraged to move ahead in trying to help her.

1. Her problems aren't caused by a medical situation or disturbed state, but she does need support. I may need to help her sort out the dilemma, but she mainly needs me to listen.

2. Her problems aren't medical or psychological in nature, but she needs suggestions on how to cope with her current crisis. Since I have experienced this directly or indirectly, I can share and help.

3. This individual is under great stress. Life is less happy or productive than it could be, and I believe I could teach her some skills which would help—such as parenting, time management, dealing with guilt, etc.

4. Her problem appears to be a spiritual one, which I have experienced directly or indirectly—lack of a consistent and vibrant prayer life, for instance, or heaping expectations upon my husband instead of God. Are her spiritual moorings tied tightly? Does she perhaps lack true understanding of the Christian life as God wants it lived?

HOW DO I MOVE INTO A COUNSELING RELATIONSHIP?

In all of my discipling relationships only a handful of serious predicaments have surfaced immediately. Often a surprisingly deep-rooted problem required neither the intense therapy or involvement of a genuine counseling situation. Instead, it called for the everyday kind of nurturing we've explored in this book.

What follows is a list of insights that have been helpful to me when a woman I've been discipling needs counseling.

1. If you have chosen to meet specifically to talk about the problem, as I did with Stephanie, be sure you have set time limits. Make sure your friend is aware of them. Then hear out her problem, but don't encourage a woman to open up further than you are prepared to help.

2. Look for patterns and listen intently. Ask yourself, "What is she *feeling*?" I've sometimes needed to help a woman express her feelings by asking, "What most distresses you today?" This also narrows into a workable size what could turn out to be the "whole dump truck load" of past and present problems.

3. Clarify her problem ("It sounds as if you feel . . .") and the facts in a nonjudgmental way, using Scripture.

4. Clarify your own limits. What do you expect to do within this relationship?

5. Let her know that she must make the final choices—choices about what she is not going to do, as well as choices about what she is going to do. She must assume a responsibility for her own actions and attitudes and decisions.

6. Determine goals. What does she want and expect to see changed within the next few days, weeks, months? How will she accomplish this? Define and examine each alternative to the apparent solutions in the light of biblical standards, the young woman's values, and long-range goals.

7. As you conclude your time together, encourage her to choose one alternative, then tell her how you will help her in planning a series of steps to carry out her decision. These actions will be her homework, to bridge the days until you next get together.

8. Assure her of your acceptance and availability and prayer support. Pray with her about her problem.

Although I sometimes set aside the discipling recipe to concentrate on an urgent problem, whenever possible I continue with the mix of praise, encouragement, prayer, and study. She needs this balanced diet to be a healthier person.

How Do I Balance Counseling with Discipling?

WHAT ARE SOME COMMON PROBLEMS?

Loneliness. I've discovered that many women appear to have their act together and to have the variables of their lives flying in the same direction, but in reality they feel incredibly lonely. Loneliness may be the most painful wound the human heart can experience.

The simple words I saw on a poster in a church hallway express a deep truth: "People are lonely because they build walls instead of bridges." Perhaps we older women need to add "bridge building" to our mentoring job description!

Erich Fromm writes, "The deepest need of man is the need to overcome his separateness, to leave the prison of his aloneness."[1] Next to our universal need for peace with God, I believe overcoming that separateness tops our "want lists," whether we know it or not.

Father/Daughter Relationship. I've counseled many women about their relationships with their fathers. Usually a woman's attitude toward God ties in closely with the relationship she enjoyed (or did not enjoy) with her earthly father.

Shelley reinforced what I felt and gradually heard from other sources: a woman's perspective of herself as a woman, her feelings about being a woman, are closely tied to how her father treated her. There is a deep need to "please daddy" and to know that he likes having a girl child/woman; there is a yearning for his love to be demonstrated and verbalized.

Shelley's dad told her she couldn't do much or excel in most things because she was a girl. And he apparently favored her brother. What seemed more devastating to Shelley was the change from their earlier closeness. She had adored her dad as a child, but he turned away and distanced himself emotionally when she reached junior high age. Perhaps he didn't understand or he feared the woman he saw emerging in his daughter. Shelley's puberty was a very unhappy time, partly because of her frustration and anger at not being a boy. For almost thirty years Shelley has tried to please and to anticipate the feelings and reactions of any man in her life.

Our childhood experiences strongly influence our ability to affirm ourselves and others. Most of us respond in the same ways we responded as we grew up—perhaps with hopelessness, or judgmentally, or defensively, or negatively.

Sometimes I need to tell my young friend that God is not like her own father. Then we study in the Gospels about the nature of Jesus, who told the disciples that if they learned to know Him they would also know what the Heavenly Father was like (chapters 14-16 of John's gospel).

Misplaced Mothering. The mothering instinct becomes a beautiful quality within the setting of marriage and family, but some single women are controlled by this desire to nurture others.

Usually a young man plays on her sympathy ("nobody else understands me"), perhaps intentionally, perhaps not. Without realizing what is happening, the young woman feels sorry for him; she wants to mother and help him. Few young women recognize this drive in themselves, so we who are their role models and spiritual moms should create an awareness of this potential danger zone.

Most women have a deep desire to give themselves away and to be needed, but I want to do my best to see that no one takes advantage of the vulnerability and loving nature of the young women I disciple.

CHEERING AND CONFRONTING

With each insight I've mentioned, I've recognized in a fresh way the value of giving accepting, affirming, and encouraging strokes. Sad to say, we may be the only cheering section this young woman can claim at this point in her life.

Between the time the problem first shows its face and the next time we get together, I keep in close contact. Women (as you and I both know!) have a built-in need to talk with someone who cares. I've found that some women think they need counseling when all they really need is consistent nurturing from a gifted listener.

How Do I Balance Counseling with Discipling?

Last autumn I wrote in my journal:

Shelley called, unsettled by advice from friends who feel she ought to 'lay it on the line' with Dale. After we talked a while, Shelley commented on how much it meant just to know I 'was there'; that she needed the perspective of someone other than her peers.

My fellow-discipler Evelyn confirms my suspicion that many young women—especially those with deep and continuing problems—already feel buffeted by the people in their lives telling them "do this" and "don't do that." They don't want more free advice. These individuals will come across as especially sensitive when you and I suggest too much, too often. These women will sometimes appear to ignore our well-intentioned recommendations. That may be the time to "just be there" for them. Given the freedom to make her own choice, your mentoring partner may surprise you by a sudden decisiveness in her own time.

Coupled with this affirmation and availability must come the willingness to exhort, to confront, and to keep her accountable. Every woman I've had a lay counseling relationship with has lacked this vital ingredient of accountability. Before you groan and reply, "We've already talked about that," let me emphasize again the importance of this concept. Unless we are women set apart from the rest, you and I have unrelenting blind spots about ourselves. We need the help of someone who opens the door wide enough for us to glimpse our real selves. As they lovingly hold us accountable for our actions, words, attitudes, promises, and goals, we gain valuable insights into ourselves.

The discipler-equipper must at times ask "why?" She must ask the other woman to define what she should be doing and should not be doing. And, in demanding accountability, she must herself have qualifying traits of authenticity, availability, honesty, confidentiality, objectivity, and godliness.

Notice Paul's example of confronting as he put his good-byes into words for the Ephesian elders:

You know how I lived the whole time I was with you, from the first day I came . . . You know that I have not hesitated to preach anything that would be helpful to you. . . . So be on your guard! Remember that for three years I never stopped warning each of you night and day with tears. (Acts 20:18, 20, 31)

Paul's discipling-counseling pattern is true for today. You and I are to *spend time* with our young women; to *train and teach* them about everything that pertains to their lives; to *warn* and *confront* them; to allow ourselves, within reasonable limits, to *become vulnerable*, even emotionally and spiritually tied to these women ("night and day with tears").

KNOWING OUR LIMITS

A counselor must not carry the problems of other women beyond their time together, except in prayer. And we must not feel personally responsible for changes as they happen—or don't happen—in the life of the young woman.

A spiritual mentor sets her personal involvement-in- counseling limits early on, then regularly asks herself how well she is staying within those limits. She knows that her own situation must detail the degree of her responsibility. What feels quite appropriate for me with my current circumstances may seem very unrealistic for you at this time.

We also need to know our abilities and limits well enough to know whether we should refer our disciple to a professional. We definitely must refer when:

- She has lost contact with reality or has delusions. For example, she believes someone is following her or is out to get her when no one is.

- The same emotions which most of us experience to some degree show up in exaggerated forms such as: deep depression, extreme mood swings, compulsions (about safety, cleanliness, perfection).

- Chronic behavior patterns appear more serious or less open to change than you believed at first.

- Strong aggressiveness is noted in attitudes, speech, thoughts, actions.

- False guilt builds up; she feels guilty when she ought not to, sometimes continuing to struggle with the guilt after asking for forgiveness.

- She lacks the ability to think about the consequences of what she does and can't mentally put herself in the place of someone else.

- She threatens suicide.

- Dependence on drugs or any chemical substance is confirmed.

- You see no changes in the problem or situation after several months of nurturing and counseling. She doesn't seem to be trying to get better, but only wants to feel better.

- You realize that you are being used or manipulated.

- Physical symptoms are intense and of long duration or seem abnormal. The referral should be to a medical doctor.

All but the last of these situations need referral to a Christian psychiatrist. I specify the kind of psychiatrist because only a Christian counselor will consider the importance of biblical values. And don't hesitate to refer; it is better to err in that direction than in *not* referring.

In addition to asking a Christian medical doctor for a referral or the name of a board-certified Christian psychiatrist, most pastors stay well informed about sources for this kind of help. Find out also what resources are available through your own church and nearby churches. Many medium to large-sized churches have counselors on staff.

The county health division can also be contacted. City and county resources are detailed in frequently updated brochures.

Every potential counselor should track these down to have on hand before the crisis hits.

Special conferences and seminars may offer excellent peer counseling workshops. I've gleaned "how to" and needed tools from five or six of these workshops in my area in recent years. And I intend to continue updating my people-helping skills as the opportunities arise.

My long-range objective is to feel comfortably confident when the discipling develops into stressful problem-solving which is within my limits and capabilities.

LOOKING BACK, LOOKING AHEAD

As I reflect on the long-range results of my involvement with Stephanie, I admit that the changes weren't what I'd hoped for originally. Her marriage eventually ended, but I feel that Stephanie gave it her best and learned to give more of her expectations over to her Lord. She practiced patience, trusting in God, adjusting—qualities which weren't previously her natural bent.

God is able to heal the hurts and emotional problems, but He sometimes doesn't do this because He knows we are more empathetic, more useful to others as one of God's wounded healers.

> Our wounds are the visa into the country of another person's deep being.... In sharing our wounds, the healing power is released. We learn that he who would bind another's wounds must allow his own wounds to be bound. God has only one kind of healer in this world—a wounded healer....
>
> Our primary task in our life together is not to take away pain but to deepen it to a level where it can be shared. In the sharing is the healing. We are not to be ashamed of our wounds nor proud of them, but simply willing to acknowledge them and to share them and to recognize them as signs of hope.[2]

MORE WORTHY WOMAN IDEAS

1. Read one or more of the resource books listed below (or one listed in the footnotes), then list a few points from that book which could prove helpful to you or someone else in the future.

> Collins, Gary. *How to Help a Friend*. Wheaton, Ill.: Tyndale House Publishers, 1983.
>
> Crabb Jr., Lawrence. *Effective Biblical Counseling*. Grand Rapids, Mich.: Zondervan, 1977.
>
> Mains, Karen Burton. *The Key To a Loving Heart*. Elgin, Ill.: David C. Cook, 1979.
>
> Seamands, David. *Healing for Damaged Emotions*. Wheaton, Ill.: Victor Books, 1981.
>
> Welter, Paul. *How to Help a Friend*. Wheaton, Ill.: Tyndale House Publishers, 1983.

1. Erich Fromm, *The Art of Loving* (New York: Harper & Row, 1956), p. 8.
2. Robert Raines, *Success Is a Moving Target* (Waco, Tex.: Word Books, 1975), p. 131.

11

OTHER
QUESTIONS I'VE ASKED

MUST I DISCIPLE EVERYONE WHO ASKS?

We know that even Jesus Christ did not heal all the sick or demon-possessed or blind. But this reasonable question must have unsettled your mind at times, as it has mine. I really struggle with wanting to carry out the ministry of helping, even when I'm already going into overload.

What if your pastor telephones today to ask your help with a woman whose teenager is tearing her apart? And tomorrow

135

a note in the mail from Sandi asks if she can meet with you weekly, starting next Friday but you are already working with a young woman?

I've appreciated and put into practice some helpful thoughts along this line, from a *Partnership* magazine article by Frances White. She suggested:

> Sometimes the shoulds and oughts seem to compel us to go further than we realistically can. . . . Therefore, we function as if we should never let an opportunity to help another pass by. Yet the very concept of sovereignty implies that God's purpose will be accomplished with or without us.

This author reminds us that Jesus knew the importance of adults making their own decisions (note His encounter with the rich young ruler in Luke 18:18) and learning obedience through suffering (He knew Peter's proclamation of loyalty would turn into denial).

Then Ms. White asks, "Are we willing to let those to whom we minister suffer so they can become motivated to grow? . . . Is the energy we need for other tasks too easily consumed because we feel we always ought to hurt when another does?"[1]

That lady hit my nail right on the head!

The crux of the matter does appear to require restraining ourselves from doing for others anything they can do for themselves. I've caught myself offering to help before considering carefully my motives for volunteering so quickly. I've burdened myself unwisely and usually needlessly with a pack of "shoulds" and "oughts."

When the woman wanting discipling doesn't seem to have an immediate or urgent need, I've learned it's okay to ask about postponing our starting date. Kristin willingly waited two months, and I think the mutual anticipation added a healthy fringe benefit. I also like to suggest two or three other women whose time might become available sooner than mine.

IS DISCIPLESHIP EVER A TWO-WAY STREET?

Yes, sometimes two women become aware of a conscious and mutual mentoring of one another. Often this kind of relationship develops gradually, as mutual strengths and weaknesses emerge.

Fortunately, my weakness is often your strength. I've felt a little self-conscious all my life, but I've marveled at the way God blends my weaknesses and strengths with your different strengths and weaknesses—resulting in a healthy mixture. Sometimes the younger person becomes the stronger person, supporting the older woman for a while, giving her mentor the opportunity to lean a bit.

Last year I discovered Madeleine L'Engle's comments on the necessity of risking our ingrained complacency:

> Vulnerability is something we instinctively reject because we are taught from kindergarten on that we must protect ourselves, control our behavior and our lives. But, in becoming man for us, Christ made himself totally vulnerable for us in Jesus of Nazareth. . . .

> When we were children, we used to think that when we were grown-up we would no longer be vulnerable. But to grow up is to accept vulnerability.[2]

IS THERE REALLY ANY DIFFERENCE BETWEEN DISCIPLESHIP AND FRIENDSHIP?

This question has no simple answer because friendship does become part of a nurturing relationship. However, I believe that mentoring goes farther and deeper than most friendships. The goals and accountability and the spiritual responsibility aren't part of the usual friendship. The purpose of a mentoring relationship is for learning and change . . . most friendships aren't formed for that reason.

WHAT ABOUT THE DRY SPELLS?

I experienced a dry spell as a mentor. For two years no one asked me to disciple them, nor did I feel the Holy Spirit nudging me to initiate a relationship. I began to worry about this desert experience; I questioned the veracity of what had seemed to be an exciting and valuable ministry. Was God letting me know that my discipling days were over? Had sin or lack of spirituality prevented God from using me further?

If something blocked my spiritual arteries, I couldn't put my finger on it. So I simply decided to give to God my honest quaverings and asked Him for another spiritual daughter in His time. I hadn't lacked for worthwhile projects and people to fill my life, but I missed the inherent challenge and personal growth of each new mentoring relationship.

I can appreciate now God's wisdom in allowing the two-year drought. Somewhere in that period of time I also remembered how often Jesus needed and took time away from His ministry with people; He "withdrew again into the hills by Himself" (John 6:15). His emphasis on prayer at those times reminded me that this should also become my focus.

And as if to assure me that the dry spell was no accident, the Lord ended the dormant period by giving me two very different young women to disciple within a nine-week period.

HOW DO I ACHIEVE A BALANCED VIEW OF MYSELF?

I have to admit that mentoring relationships sometimes trigger the wrong kind of personal pride. I've used two helpful questions which act as effective antidotes for a suspected ego attack:

> Am I willing to suggest another godly mentor to a younger woman—or am I secretly convinced that I'm the only one who can do it right?

> Is mentoring becoming a "feather in my cap," rather than a genuine ministry for the Lord?

Again the Master Discipler sets the pattern. In Luke 6:17 I find that Jesus "went down with them and stood on a level place." Jesus was the one who moved down to the level where He gained equal footing with His disciples and the throng of people, rather than choosing a place above them.

IS THE RESPONSIBILITY ALL MINE?

No, the mentor isn't wholly responsible for nurturing and equipping. Growth occurs through the combined efforts of God, the disciplemaker, and the younger woman. One will plant and another will water, and the job will be completed in God's good time.

If you experience disappointment with a disciple, remember that outward change may come later. Allow God time to work. Individuals like Thomas, James, John, and Peter must have seemed like "lost causes" at one time or another during their association with their Lord.

Christie arrived unannounced at my door one afternoon. She wanted and needed help, and seemed excited as we planned ahead for some regular times together. At our first session, Christie encouraged me by the evidence of her active searching for (and finding) articles and books dealing with her particular problems. Her "first steps" appeared to be positive and creative ones.

But we've never continued the relationship past the first couple of afternoons together. Meetings have been postponed and cancelled, prompting me to feel frustrated and disappointed. What seemed like an aborted discipling attempt now looks more like a situation where the immediate need assumed greater urgency than the long-range needs.

HOW DO I KNOW WHEN TO STOP MEETING REGULARLY?

Even when you've taken to heart my suggestion of establishing a cut-off date, it is sometimes difficult to know if you should follow through. Your friend may be reluctant to break the pattern that has nurtured her, saying, "I'll miss what seems so healthy and important right now. I wish we could meet indefinitely."

I've noticed that even Paul expressed his fierce desire to be with those believers he had previously discipled. They had become very dear to him. He spoke of being away from them only a short time (though remaining close in thought), yet "Out of our intense longing we made every effort to see you. For we wanted to come to you" (1 Thessalonians 2:17-18).

You and I may occasionally experience Paul's deep feelings, but overriding our attachments will be our understanding of the importance of stretching our wings and walking worthily. God and me—on our own together.

The day will come when you will wonder, "Is this woman ready to continue without a weekly discipling group?" Or, "How do I know if my disciplemaking has 'taken' with Laura?"

Good questions. Simply put, I believe the answer is: The degree to which your younger woman turns to Scripture, and lives by it, denotes her maturity quite accurately.

I also ask myself what fruits of the Spirit I see developing in the lives of my younger friends. Do I see them moving away from themselves to stretch, to reach out, to listen to other women—to nurture and encourage them?

With a graduation card and note I've sometimes reminded young women-in-process that true maturity comes when their mirrors turn into windows. I've suspected that those thoughts were quickly forgotten.

Yet a note at the end of a Christmas card (from a thirtyish young married woman) surprised me. The comment was, "I think my mirrors have finally turned into windows!"

WHAT HAPPENS WHEN WE STOP MEETING ON A REGULAR BASIS?

Through our telephone calls, notes, and other contact points, those we've actively discipled will know they are not forgotten in the crunch of busy schedules and new commitments. After one of us declares time out for an "alumni lunch," both women receive encouragement through that face-to-face and heart-to-heart reunion.

Distances of place or time shouldn't make our close- encounters-of-the-discipling-kind any less significant or lasting. I like to keep in touch on birthdays, Christmas, when a new baby arrives, and at other special times, but don't limit myself to those occasions.

I want to find out what God is doing in my young friend's life, so I ask about her prayer needs and goals. Not trusting my often faulty memory bank, I jot down her responses so I can pray effectively. Sometimes we conclude our telephone or in-person conversation by praying together.

I also need to share myself. I've discovered and appreciated what the psalmist wrote in Psalm 79:13: "Then we your people, the sheep of your pasture, will praise you forever; from generation to generation we will recount your praise." The way you and I recount or express our praise for what God graciously does in our lives contributes to the "ripples" of ongoing support our graduate disciples need to experience.

Whenever possible, I've encouraged the younger woman to think in terms of a team ministry with her husband. Sometimes this means enhancing his home Bible study leadership. For Caryn it meant working with her husband as he advised and led the junior high kids at church. Elise helped her husband after school when he coached high school athletic teams. In addition to lots of verbal support and enthusiasm, Elise assisted her husband on excursions (team playoffs and such), and co-hosted pizza or taco feeds at their home—sometimes accompanied by a brief and voluntary Bible study. Both women put to excellent use the worthy-woman skills and attitudes learned in their small discipling group.

But for Lila (and others who don't have that kind of relationship with their husbands) the suggestion was simple and "unreligious": Choose one area where you can team up and reach out together—perhaps working a booth together at the school flea market or supervising the high school car wash.

WHAT GUIDELINES COULD I SUGGEST
TO SOMEONE LOOKING FOR A MENTOR?

In the beginning of this book I included part of my letter from Marni. Her letter also mentioned her personal guidelines for selecting a discipler. Marni wanted a woman with:

1. Maturity

2. Experience in marriage, especially in loving her husband well.

3. Earned respect, someone who was credible as a Christian and a wife.

Perhaps your friend would mutter at this point, "I wish I could be as calm and logical as this Marni, but—hey—I don't know what I want."

Let me suggest hat she compile a list of qualities she wants as part of her character ten or fifteen years from now. Her list might include selflessness and consistency; or self-confidence and a strong touch of humor.

Then you can add to that list the values that you see as really important to her. Do her values lie more in the direction of family and church traditions or are they centered closely around job success and individual growth? Does she value most her times of solitude or her times with other people?

This brief exercise will help her sort through her own values and find a woman who embraces the personal characteristics she admires and wants to pursue. Usually an everyday sort of woman works best. Someone who is part of the younger woman's church family or neighborhood, and who wants to teach what she has learned in her years as a woman.

If this woman is open to a discipling relationship and the two of them look forward to getting together soon, I suggest that the younger woman write down what she sees as two or three weaknesses in this older friend. Doing this allows her a more objective and realistic perspective on her role model in the weeks ahead. She is not perfect, and never wants to be viewed as some kind of superwoman or heroine.

WHO DISCIPLES THE MENTOR?

Mentors are shaped and nourished by those who model the qualities they respect and require for their own spiritual growth. I can mentally tick off at least six women's names (plus many who are now with the Lord) whom I look to as role rodels. Some are younger, some have lived longer thar. I have, but each one adds a valuable dimension to my life.

One woman's unselfishness motivates me to put less stock in my own puny plans. I draw upon another woman's Bible-centered lifestyle. And on it goes. Perhaps God wants us to have several role models, so we won't focus too strongly on the mentor, while becoming less dependent on the most important One, Jesus Christ.

The older I get, the more I observe that you and I become motivated by different women at different stages of our lives. That's why every one of us can mentor and equip someone. One at a time or in a small group you will make an incredible difference for certain women who wouldn't ask me for the time of day . . . let alone remember it.

Most importantly, the Holy Spirit is our discipler. Sometimes I forget that reassuring precept in my search for answers. Perhaps I've passed too quickly over a bedrock fact: Without the gentle nudging and guidance of the Holy Spirit, my disciplemaking days would end abruptly.

The Holy Spirit, the "one called alongside," enables me to come alongside a young woman who needs mentoring, equipping, and exhorting. I am able to fill this "job description," supporting and sometimes confronting that discipling partner, because of the Spirit.

HOW DO I HANDLE THE GENERATION GAP?

America stands almost alone as a country which venerates youth and pushes aside older people. But God intends for older women and men to live useful lives; He wants their years of experience to count as a valuable resource.

After the memorial service for a charter member of our church, I visited quietly with a ninety-two-year-old friend who remarked, "When an old person dies, it's like a small library going up in smoke. So much is forever lost."

Some women have confided that they feel out of touch with the rapidly changing American scene. They feel old-fashioned and a little afraid about the kind of vulnerability and honesty expected today.

What to do?

1. For just a few hours a week try reading in general interest, news, or women's magazines. And don't skip the articles on parenting and marriage and careers; the ones you think don't apply to you. Your public library can provide a broader spectrum of· magazines than those coming into your home or church library. Learn to skim a variety of topics (noting especially the ones touching on current trends and problems to push your mind into gear for good communication with younger women).

2. Involve yourself in something new. Try moving from status-quo living to a lifestyle brightened by new ideas and activities. All three of our children began their public school years with Susan Eastman's kindergarten class. Year after year, Miss Eastman communicated excitement to her pupils, blessing them with her constant creativity and curiosity.

I remember talking with her after school one day, and getting pumped up myself about her new interest. This little lady (she must have touched age sixty about then) was learning all kinds of bird calls in her ornithology night course.

She had also learned to yodel. Her eyes sparkled like a birthday child's as she demonstrated!

Bird calls and yodeling may not be your cup of tea, but I urge you to find some new sport or hobby or interest. How about studying the many uses of herbs and how to grow them? Put your family tree together or compile your family's personal history. Volunteer to host international students for a month, or to work at the hospital each Wednesday. A flock of possible activities wait in the wings for my attention and yours.

Look for a course or class you've always wanted to take. My friend Wauline and her husband took a community college course in restoring old trunks. She had a great time rescuing their family heirloom from dusty oblivion. Marilyn is learning conversational Norwegian as the first step toward a long-desired visit to the country of her parents' roots.

My next adventure into new territory will involve personal computer skills. Although I'm intimidated by the computer's foreign vocabulary and logic, I realize the importance of over-coming my negative attitude toward electronic-age tools.

3. Frequent places where you'll talk and work with younger women. This provides almost instant on-the-job training for mentoring and will help you step into their world more easily. Calligraphy class or another community college course quickly peels away the years. Listen up in these places. What new-to-your-ear expressions do you hear? What topics? What choices are young women being confronted with today?

I've enjoyed helping in our church's baby nursery. In greeting the young parents and lifting little ones from their arms, I have unlimited opportunities to get acquainted with an age group I might otherwise miss out on.

You may be better suited to teaching in children's Sunday school or working in their churchtime program. The younger children's departments always need extra grandmas as huggers and listeners.

Although we want to avoid a generation gap, I believe in an appropriate break between the generations. Titus 2:3-5 does not tell older women ". . . to teach what is good, and to be a pal to the younger women." Most of these women already have peer group friends. What they need and want is a role model, someone to be their "resource person," and to hold them accountable.

They want someone who can help them grow and stretch to become all God wants them to be.

Other Questions I've Asked

More Worthy Women Ideas

1. Can you look back to someone who seemingly disappointed you in your nurturing efforts but later showed godly growth? If this example encourages you now, why not start a "Reassurance Record Book"? Keep here the positive feedback you receive from time to time (notes, spoken words, "eyewitness accounts," etc.), then replay that pat on the back or the sound of applause as you look at these encouraging flashbacks. Good anti-discouragement "pills"!

2. Write your own prayer for those women for whom you feel a spiritual responsibility, using something like Colossians 1:9-17 or Ephesians 1:15-19 as a pattern. Be specific and personal.

3. If you feel out of touch with today's younger women, make your own list of ways to diminish any generation gap. Which will you begin with?

4. Read Deuteronomy 4:1-9. Note the details of living with a three-generation perspective, as Moses suggests.

1. Frances White, "Dealing with the 'I Must Help Everyone' Syndrome," *Partnership*, May/June 1984, p. 10, 12.
2. Madeleine L'Engle, *Walking on Water* (Wheaton, Ill.: Harold Shaw Publishers, 1980), pp. 189-190.

12

ARE YOU WILLING TO BECOME A WOMAN OF INFLUENCE?

———————————————

I had no idea that someday Mrs. Parker would rank a chronological first in my personal "Role Model Hall of Fame." My mind only recalls her outward appearance as "pleasantly plump," in accord with my mother's polite phrase.

Mrs. Parker seemed ordinary—except for her outrageous, radical idea that God really and truly answers prayer!

In the late 1930s Christians used stained-glass language that kept Jesus Christ at a safe, impersonal distance. They rationalized away any true commitment by saying that

149

Christianity would automatically show through their lives. Adelaide Parker was the first adult I remember (except for the preacher, maybe, but I'm not even sure about him) who easily and continually verbalized her love relationship with Jesus Christ! She openly lived and spoke her beliefs.

My Sunday school teacher told us about praying before shopping at the "Friday Surprise" sales at Meier and Frank department store. In those post-Depression years, money for clothing was hard to come by. Her enthusiasm sparkled as she wore (or described to us later) the dress she found for the exact amount of her saved-up cash—sometimes $5.00, sometimes as much as $7.25.

Mrs. Parker told us about other amazing and direct answers to prayer. She endangered our complacency by coming right out and talking about God. And about her faith—on weekdays and outside the church building!

I remember thinking that a life lived with that kind of certainty and faith was the kind of adult life I wanted. In later years I would wistfully recall the enthusiasm of Mrs. Parker's obedient, joyful life and shiver a bit as I wished for the warmth of her relationship with God.

Last month I found the little plaque she gave each of "her girls," as they moved on to the next Sunday school class. The words "Prayer Changes Things" sounded less old-fashioned now than I remembered them sounding in my high school and college years.

I'll always be grateful for the indelible heartprint this dear lady made upon my life. She modeled for me the peace and contentment that comes from praying about the daily events of our lives.

Along the way other women (and a few men) jostled the shyness and immaturity which inhibited my growth in Jesus Christ. And, at the same time, they nurtured and drew forth the finer, deeper qualities God intended for me all along.

Three cheers and a round of applause for the encouragers—for those special people who have influenced our lives so incredibly!

Because you and I have gained from others we need to look inward and ask ourselves how we are influencing the women whose lives we will closely touch during our lifetime. We must be God's women in our own particular web of relationships.

Queen Esther seized the opportunity to dramatically influence the political mess in her own country. "And who knows but that you have come to the kingdom for such a time as this and for this very occasion?" (Esther 4:14, Amplified).

Few of us would want Esther's unusual opportunity. But the principle distilled from her experience is clear: Each of us can make a difference in our unique mini-world.

GOD'S GREAT IDEA FOR WOMEN

I was reminded (at a time when I felt smugly content) that a ship anchored in the harbor is safe—but that's not what ships are for. For many of us, growing older whets our appetite mostly for safety and comfort. But that's not what God had in mind when He created us!

Have you tasted and felt the substance of disciplemaking as you've read this book? I hope so, because I also want your heart and mind to rejoice in the continuing influence which goes on for generations through the gracious work of the Holy Spirit.

"Lord, you have assigned me my portion and my cup; you have made my lot secure. The boundary lines have fallen for me in pleasant places; surely I have a delightful inheritance" (Psalm 16:5-6).

The Amplified version gives verse six as "yes, I have a good heritage." The NASB translates this as "Indeed, my heritage is beautiful to me." And the Living Bible exclaims, "What a wonderful inheritance!"

For this season of my life, I believe the portion and cup the Lord has assigned to me is nurturing and discipling younger women. And many of you will also catch the desire to become part of this satisfying ministry. Although I initially approached discipling with caution, it has become my refreshing cup, overflowing with pleasure, and my fulfilling portion of God's goodness.

God has made my lot (my place in His world) completely secure. I no longer need the Linus-style security blanket I clutched for so many years as a child of the Great Depression.

Although the adjustment of lifestyle and schedule required by these nurturing relationships does place some boundary lines around my public and personal life, God always places those limits in pleasant places. Without God's boundaries, I might have missed knowing young ladies like Janelle and Karen and Marni and Shelley and the rest. I might have never experienced the joy and the early taste of "eternal pleasures" (Psalm 16:11) which our Heavenly Father has lovingly planned for His older children.

Have you glimpsed the personal satisfaction, the challenge of nurturing younger women according to God's wise precepts in chapter 2 of Titus? And have you younger women taken a tentative step toward learning about the ways of a godly woman, from a mentor's life?

Linda Anderson wrote about her mentor:

> And she fostered in me a desire and eventually an ability to overflow into someone else's life, as she had into mine. Her friendship was like a soft pillow: restorative, not demanding, and available. . . . Here was a plain-spoken woman who obviously enjoyed the Christian life. . . . Each time we were together, I studied her experience with God and learned the ground rules of Christian living. . . . Scripture taught her how to reach from her 'here' to someone else's 'there,' and to become a bridge builder, and a pathway clearer, and a light shedder—as if it were second nature to her.[1]

Sounds like this woman initiated quite a few ripples of influence!

Are You Willing to Become a Woman of Influence?

The apostle Paul asked in 1 Thessalonians 2:19, "For what is [my] hope, our joy, or the crown in which we will glory in the presence of our Lord Jesus when He comes? Is it not you? Indeed, you are our glory and joy."

Imagine—only one or two disciples in a lifetime may become your glory and joy, from generation to generation!

MORE WORTHY WOMAN IDEAS

1. Are you willing right now to ask God about investing in future generations by nurturing a young woman, one He continues to bring to your mind? Or, as a younger woman, are you willing to seek out a mentor?

2. Select one of the books from the "recommended" list at the back of this book. Read it for your own benefit, as well as with the idea of passing it on to another woman, asking for her thoughts on the author's ideas.

3. Have you written that note of appreciation to one or more individuals who influenced your life at some point?

---

1. Linda Anderson, "Aunt Jane, The Mentor," *Today's Christian Woman*, May/June 1986, p.46.

APPENDIX A

Topics and Books for Study

TOPICS

1. What is a "disciplined life"? How do we have one?
2. Maintaining good attitudes under pressure.
3. Building good friendships and keeping them.
4. Happy husband guidelines—no one can assist and affirm a husband better than his wife.
5. Role and identity struggles.
6. Communication skills.
7. Spiritual gifts and women's ministry/role in the local church.
8. Financial guidelines. Giving to the church and other

Christian organizations; budgeting; faith and finances—how much of the world's "security" is appropriate for believers?

Special women bring special needs to the nurturing relationship. Some one-time requests have included:

1. What to look for in a mate.
2. Regaining a "fresh joy" in knowing the Lord.
3. Resisting sexual temptations.
4. Knowing God's will.

BOOKS

Alexander, Pat. *The Lion Encyclopedia of the Bible*. Batavia, Ill.: Lion Publishing, 1986.

Deen, Edïth. *All the Women of the Bible*. New York: Harper & Brothers, 1955.

Gaebelein, Frank E., ed. *The Expositor's Bible Commentary*, vol. 8. Grand Rapids, Mich.: Zondervan, 1984.

Goodrick, Edward W. and Kohlenberger III, John R. *The NIV Complete Concordance*. Grand Rapids, Mich.: Zondervan, 1981.

Hillyer, N., ed. *The New Bible Dictionary* rev. ed. Wheaton, Ill.: Tyndale House Publishers, 1982.

Karssen, Gien. *Her Name Is Woman*, [Books I & II]. Colorado Springs, Colo.: NavPress, 1975, 1977.

Meredith, J.L. *Meredith's Book of Bible Lists*. Minneapolis, Minn.: Bethany Books, 1982.

Richards, Lawrence O. *The Word Bible Handbook*. Waco, Tex.: Word Books, 1982.

Tenney, Merrill C., ed. *The Zondervan Pictorial Encyclopedia of the Bible*. Grand Rapids, Mich.: Zondervan, 1975.

Unger, Merrill E., ed. *Unger's Bible Handbook*. Chicago, Ill.: Moody Press, 1966.

Vine, W.E. *An Expository Dictionary of New Testament Words*. Old Tappan, N.J.: Fleming H. Revell, 1940.

Young, Robert, ed. *Young's Analytical Concordance to the Bible*. Grand Rapids, Mich.: Wm. E. Eerdmans, 1964.

APPENDIX B

An Old Testament Role Model

Solomon's thumbnail sketch of the Proverbs 31 woman describes a "wife of noble character." I'm impressed with how greatly she is valued by her husband and I note the complete confidence he feels in his wife. His heart trusts in her and knows her commitment is for his good. "She brings him good, not harm, all the days of her life" (Proverbs 31:12).

Because of his wife's godly qualities, he is "respected at the city gate" (v. 23). This woman basks in the outspoken, loving approval of her husband and her children (v. 28), something many women desire year after year.

Our Proverbs woman appears to have learned well the precepts of Titus 2:3-5, although we have no record of her as a disciple or a disciplemaker. Instead, I suspect that God shows us in Proverbs 31 the kind of worthy woman He wants both younger and older women to look for in a role model.

Discussing and studying this woman's qualities could provide rich material for several discipling sessions. Consider her:

1. Spiritual strength. Her actions and lifestyle reflect her faith (vv. 10, 25, 30); her words of wisdom are rooted in her relationship to God (v. 26); her kindness and works, shown by the way she helps the needy (v. 20) demonstrate her love for God.

2. Vocational achievement. She busily prepares food and clothing for her family; she gardens and sews (vv. 13-16, 19). She is also a professional woman (vv. 16, 24), proving herself to be enterprising, resourceful, and creative. Her achievements come from a heart attitude of joyful service, not financial or peer pressure. In addition to her own real estate ventures, she undoubtedly listened carefully to her husband's business opinions and decisions.

3. Resourcefulness. Verses 21 and 25 show this woman's adaptability to different situations. She is a mover. Perhaps a shaker, too, if rugs graced her home! She was appropriately, healthily involved with her home and community.

4. Social grace. She knows about relating well to others in her marital relationship (v. 11), with her children (v. 27), and to those outside the family (v. 20). Our worthy woman extends the boundaries of her home by sharing material blessings with others.

5. Inner Beauty. This Proverbs 31 woman dresses discreetly (v. 22). I see her as well dressed and well groomed, but outward appearance is not her top priority. Her outside glow reflects inner peace, contentment, and beauty.

This godly woman displays all of these qualities woven together into the fabric of her lifestyle. Her reward (v. 31) isn't a small or shabby thing.

ONE ROLE MODEL FROM THE NEW TESTAMENT

Mary's relationship with her cousin Elizabeth suggests that Jesus' mother looked to her older cousin's example. In the beginnings of Mary's pregnancy, she sought out the person she could best share her heart with, and then she stayed with Elizabeth for three months.

Mary must have delighted in staying with this older, experienced woman whom she respected and loved. She must have asked endless questions about having babies and caring for them. Surely some choice nurturing went on.

APPENDIX C

Additional Homework Assignments

The following examples of homework I've given may stimulate ideas you can use in your own mentoring experience.

- Begin reading *The Friendship Factor.* List the qualities you look for in friends and evaluate your own friendships. What ways can you work to make them better? Following chapter twelve I've listed other books I've assigned as supplementary reading. Add your own favorites to the list. The joy of reading should become as contagious as January's flu virus!)

- Read Psalm 139 and Isaiah 43:1-3 each night this week before going to sleep. Then take one positive action which places your humanity, fears, struggles, and ups and downs beneath God's sovereignty. Let me know what happened when we get together next week.

- Write down the qualities you think are essential for a woman of excellence, a godly or worthy woman. Then read Proverbs 31:10-31, Titus 2:3-5, and Philippians 2:3 before adding to your list some of God's ideas.

- Focus continually on Jesus Christ and "things of good report" this week. Read Colossians 3:12-17, Galatians 5:1, and Isaiah 43:18-19. Then find another verse of Scripture which helps you to keep your thoughts on the Lord and on the good aspects of life around you.

- List all the reasons you think hospitality counts as a ministry, then all the ways you can think of to make it an enjoyable and easier ministry. Let's share our lists next week and look at God's perspective on the subject. Start reading *Open Heart, Open Home* by Karen Mains.

- Choose one trait for which God is often praised and write your own psalm, praising God for His act of (chosen trait) in your life.

- This week look for a specific insight or example of God's guidance during the three weeks we've been together. What Scripture affirms this?

- Spend time praying, asking the Lord to show you how to make His Word a more essential part of your life. What might you have to give up in order to make this a reality? Share your conclusions in two weeks as we set up a systematic program of Bible study.

- Read the Book of Ruth and note on paper the "godly woman" qualities you spot.

- Think back through your life and write down the ways God has helped you to have victory over specific problems or habits. What biblical principles were involved?

- Finish writing your personal goals chart, including the short-, mid-, and long-range goals. Bring them next time, and decide how you will plan now to achieve your six-months goals. Read Romans 7:15-25 and Proverbs 16:9.

Homework could also take the shape of (1) interviewing another person, (2) observing a particular ministry, (3) encouraging friendship-building with a non-Christian co-worker (4) listing twenty caring, creative ways to demonstrate love for our husbands (and carrying out at least five of them).

SUGGESTED READING

Alexander, Myrna. *Behold Your God.* Grand Rapids, Mich.: Zondervan Publishing House, 1983.

Augsburger, David. *Caring Enough to Hear.* Ventura, Calif.: Regal Books, 1982.

Baker, Don. *Acceptance: Loosing the Webs of Personal Insecurity.* Portland, Ore.: Multnomah Press, 1985.

Collins, Gary. *How to Be a People Helper.* Santa Ana, Calif.: Vision House, 1976.

Suggested Reading

Curran, Dolores. *Traits of a Healthy Family*. Minneapolis: Winston Seabury Press, 1983.

Duckworth, Marion. *Becoming Complete: Embracing Your Biblical Image*. Portland, Ore.: Multnomah Press, 1985.

Elliot, Elisabeth. *Let Me Be a Woman*. Wheaton: Tyndale House Publishers, 1976.

Gibson, Eva. *Intimate Moments*. San Bernardino, Calif.: Here's Life Publishers, 1986.

Heald, Cynthia. *Becoming a Woman of Excellence*. Colorado Springs: NavPress, 1986.

Hendricks, Jeanne. *A Woman for All Seasons*. Nashville: Thomas Nelson Publishers, 1977.

_____. *Afternoon*. Nashville: Thomas Nelson Publishers, 1977.

Herr, Ethel L. *Bible Study for Busy Women*. Chicago: Moody Press, 1982.

Karssen, Gien. *Her Name Is Woman*. (Books I & II) Colorado Springs: NavPress, 1975, 1977.

Lindbergh, Anne Morrow. *Gift from the Sea*. New York: Random House Publishers, 1955.

Mainhood, Beth. *Reaching Your World: Disciplemaking for Women*. Colorado Springs: NavPress, 1986.

Lucado, Max. *No Wonder They Call Him Savior*. Portland, Ore.: Multnomah Press, 1986.

McGinnis, Alan Loy. *The Friendship Factor*. Minneapolis: Augsburg, 1979.

McMinn, Gordon and Libby, Larry. *Choosing to Be Close*. Portland, Ore.: Multnomah Press, 1984.

Ortlund, Anne. *Disciplines of a Beautiful Woman*. Waco, Tex.: Word Books, 1977.

Pippert, Rebecca Manley. *Out of the Saltshaker*. Downers Grove, Ill.: InterVarsity Press, 1979.

Seamands, David. *Healing for Damaged Emotions*. Wheaton: Victor Books, 1981.

Welter, Paul. *How to Help a Friend*. Wheaton: Tyndale House Publishers, 1978.

Wright, Norman H. *Seasons of a Marriage*. Ventura, Calif.: Regal Books, 1982.